Lichens of the North Woods

Lichens
of the North Woods

By Joe Walewski

Kollath+Stensaas
P U B L I S H I N G

Kollath+Stensaas Publishing
394 Lake Avenue South, Suite 406
Duluth, MN 55802
Office: 218.727.1731
Orders: 800.678.7006
info@kollathstensaas.com
www.kollathstensaas.com

LICHENS *of the* NORTH WOODS

Printed in Canada by Friesens
10 9 8 7 6 5 4 3 2

Editorial Director: Mark Sparky Stensaas
Graphic Designer: Rick Kollath

Illustrations by Rick Kollath, Kollath Graphic Design
Cartoon on page 5 by Billy Anderson

ISBN 13: 978-0-9792006-0-1

Table of Contents

To Lori & Jenny,
Together we can make anything possible.

Acknowledgements

Anyone who has ever completed a project like this knows how difficult it is to acknowledge everyone who had a role in the final product. Do I start with thanking my parents? Well, sure. They set me squarely on the path that eventually led to this point. I don't imagine that any of us ever gives enough credit to our parents. Thanks Mom and Dad.

Then, my wife, Lori, and daughter, Jenny, played vital roles throughout every step of the process. Both asked thoughtful questions and accompanied me on many searches. They made me feel important and helped me to justify all the time I spent working on the book. I also spent hundreds of hours alone in the woods, library and office while the two of them happily kept the rest of my life in order.

There are so many others who deserve credit; here are some of the highlights.

Rick Naaktgeboren opened my eyes to the botanical world by pausing, while repairing one of the tractors I'd broken, to show me a blooming sulfur cinquefoil. Terry McLaughlin, B.J. and John Kohlstedt, Peter Harris, Peter Smerud and Jack Pichotta mentored me as a growing naturalist. Lynden Gerdes modeled a sense of wonder and sensitivity that I hope to pass on to every student I encounter. Kurt Mead motivated me to try something beyond what I thought possible. Bruce Munson conveyed his confidence in me. Cliff Wetmore, Ted Esslinger and Tami McDonald offered lichen expertise and more encouragement.

Finally, I want to thank all of the student naturalists who have passed through Wolf Ridge Environmental Learning Center. You inspire me daily in so many ways.

This book made it to your hands because of these and many other marvelous people. I thank them all.

Joe Walewski
May 6, 2007

We at Kollath-Stensaas thank Joe for his full involvement in the book making process. His passion for lichens and his appreciation of deadlines has made this book a pleasure to put together.

The Publishers; Mark Sparky Stensaas, Rick Kollath
May 16, 2007

The Wide World of Lichens

Welcome to the Lilliputian world of lichens! Time and again, I hear students saying, "Wow, I've never seen things like this before." But we have seen them. Lichens are right in front of our eyes. Everywhere. In my backyard, many of the tree trunks are so completely covered in lichens that each square inch may have four or five different species. A single Sugar Maple may be a home to as many as twenty lichen species tree-wide. In one of those pure moments of awareness, a friend asked, "so what does the bark look like?"

A single Sugar Maple can be covered with as many as twenty species of lichens.

John Muir was right when he wrote: "When you tug on a single thing in nature you find it attached to the entire universe." Whether you study birds, moose, insects, soils, people, chemistry, environmental issues, arts or medicine, you'll find lichens in the mix. They are so ubiquitous, yet so small; it's no surprise that many people inadvertently overlook them. Lichens are perhaps the most "obvious" overlooked component of our landscape.

Many animals utilize lichens at some point in their lives. Ruby-throated Hummingbirds use Shield Lichens (*Parmelia*) in nest construction for camouflage. Northern Parula Warblers construct nests by weaving strands of draping Beard Lichens (*Usnea*). Spruce Grouse, White-tailed Deer, Moose and Flying Squirrels all eat lichens. Mites, springtails, bark lice, silverfish, slugs and snails dine on lichens too. Some insects and tree frogs capitalize on the camouflage provided by lichens.

Some hummingbird species use Shield Lichens (*Parmelia*) to camouflage their tiny nests.

As pioneers in a young landscape, lichens degrade rock surfaces and prepare areas for mosses, grasses and trees that follow. Species with cyanobacteria can make significant contributions to soil fertility—especially regarding usable nitrogen. All of this takes hundreds and thousands of years, but lichens patiently make their contributions.

Because lichens are highly efficient collectors of airborne substances, they fill the role of recycling airborne chemicals into the soil. Unfortunately, they can also direct heavy metals and radiation into the food chain. During the 1940s and 50s, atmospheric testing of atomic bombs introduced massive amounts of radioactive nuclides into the air. Reindeer lichens are efficient accumulators of these substances. As a result, caribou ingesting the lichens concentrated radioactive materials in their bones and tissues. Indigenous people who relied on the caribou as a food source then had an increased likelihood of bone cancer and leukemia.

In several places around the world, lichens are being used as bio-indicators of air quality. They serve as inexpensive filtering systems to monitor the spread of dirty air from factories, power plants and urban areas. In one instance in Ireland, school children were organized as citizen scientists to collect data regarding air quality around their homes. They identified those lichens living around them and plotted the information on a map. Lichen diversity was low in some areas and higher in others.

Vibrant dye colors can be created when using lichens.

The resulting maps provided compelling evidence of poor air quality closer to power plants and better air quality further from the center of urbanization. The maps even provided evidence of prevailing winds and the spread of dirty air.

Natural dyes are one of the few historical uses of lichen. The original Harris Tweed from the Harris Islands of Scotland was colored using lichens up until the 1970s. For about a fifty-year span from 1758 to 1810, the Cuthbert family in Scotland scraped Cudbear (*Ochrolechia*), for the production of a purple dye, from nearby rocks until the resource was completely depleted. Lichens grow so slowly that over harvesting is a real concern. We have not established strong economic uses for lichens…yet. Perhaps this is good.

Edibility of lichens is questionable, but possible. Starving adventurers, voyageurs and settlers ate Rock Tripe (*Umbilicaria*). Rock Tripe appears to increase in food value when boiled in several changes of water with baking soda or ashes. Northern European cultures have added ground Iceland Lichen (*Cetraria islandica*) to breads and porridges. Aboriginal peoples of the far north made a gelatinous black paste of Horsehair Lichen (*Bryoria*) shaped into biscuits for food.

Because of antibacterial and anti-germination properties, many lichen substances are being studied for sources of medicines or other beneficial uses. Iceland Moss (*Cetraria islandica*) can be found in herbal remedies for sore throat, harsh coughs and tuberculosis. It is also used in some toothpastes and deodorants. Usnic acid extracted from Beard Lichens (*Usnea*) and many other lichens may have future value in medicines as an antibiotic. Some chemicals are being studied for uses in natural herbicides.

Lichens are a fascinating piece of nature connected to many other things in the universe—sometimes quite literally. As you continue studying lichens, you will wonder at how much you missed before training your eyes to see them. It's a marvelous world out there. Enjoy!

What are Lichens?

Carl Linnaeus, the founder of taxonomy, called lichens the "poor trash of vegetation." Then, he assigned only one genus to all of lichens. Not long ago, because lichens are able to grow on bare rock with no apparent methods of reproduction or sources of nutrition, even well educated people believed they were stones caught in the process of becoming plants.

That one genus — *Lichen* — has since been expanded upon. Today, hundreds of genera and between 14,000 and 20,000 species of lichens are recognized worldwide. Science is uncovering the marvelous world of lichens. Yet, study with molecular tools is revealing a world that we become less and less sure of. The more we learn about lichens, the more we realize how much we don't know.

Freddy Fungus and Alice Algae

When I teach about lichens, I share the story of Freddy Fungus and Alice Algae to introduce students to the concept of lichens:

> *Freddy Fungus lived alone in a spacious home that he built himself. Freddy was a master architect, engineer and builder. Unfortunately, with all his skills, Freddy couldn't sustain a life alone. He was quickly fading away primarily because he just didn't take care of himself. He couldn't cook.*
>
> *Then Alice Algae came along. She seemed a magician with food. She appeared to concoct fabulous meals from nothing more than thin air. And for Alice, making food was more than a passion; it was a way of life. It became an obsession and she routinely made more than was possible to eat by herself. For, she too lived alone.*
>
> *When they first met, everyone could see they were destined to be together. True love? Maybe. All they would admit was that they immediately took a "liken" to each other. Freddy and Alice developed a relationship in which they lived symbiotically ever after.*

The story simplifies what's actually quite complex — a lichen is a unique organism composed of a fungus and an alga. But it isn't quite so simple. Lichens are actually a cooperative venture between as many as three organisms: fungus, alga and cyanobacteria. The relationship is a partnership, or symbiosis. It includes the fungus in association with at least one other organism or perhaps two. (Cybil Cyanobacteria too? We won't even go there.) Lichen fungi are never found growing alone in nature. Associated algae or cyanobacteria are most commonly found in the lichenized state, but they are occasionally found growing on their own in nature. And so the story concludes:

> *But symbiosis isn't always as you might think. Freddy and Alice didn't benefit equally. Freddy couldn't survive without Alice. Alice felt trapped*

—she couldn't be herself. As time passed, anyone could see their relationship was on the rocks.

Lichen symbiosis benefits the fungal partner most. Trevor Goward, a North American lichenologist, describes lichen as "a fungi that has discovered agriculture." Taxonomically, lichens are included in Fungi. Some scientists propose that lichens are not organisms at all, but are actually small ecosystems containing a producer (algae or cyanobacteria) and a consumer (fungus). From this perspective lichens are specialized fungi able to "lichenize." There are many other examples of specialized fungi developing vast networks of mycorrhizal associations with trees and other vascular plants. Orchids, for example, require a mycorrhizal association in order to germinate and prosper.

The evolution of lichenization is indeed very old. As early as 400 million years ago, some fungi began to develop a "lichen lifestyle" at about the same time that land plants arrived on the scene. Genetic studies show that lichenization evolved independently in many groups of fungi. There is no tight evolutionary line beginning with one single point. Consider Archaeopteryx, the fossilized creature accepted to be the evolutionary link between reptiles and birds. Lichen evolution is much more complex.

If a lichen is not an organism; if a lichen is a lifestyle; if you are still with me; then, you might realize by now that lichens are nature in miniature. Even as we zoom in on a more thorough understanding of our surroundings, we remain baffled by many seemingly simple aspects of nature. For example, lichenologists understand that lichens reproduce sexually—they have found all the appropriate parts. However, they have been unable to witness lichen sexual reproduction in the lab or nature. Lichens remain a bit of a mystery.

Lichen Biology 101

Where they grow

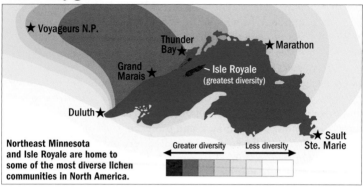

★ Voyageurs N.P.

Thunder
Bay ★

★ Marathon

Grand
Marais ★

Isle Royale
(greatest diversity)

Duluth ★

★ Sault
Ste. Marie

Northeast Minnesota and Isle Royale are home to some of the most diverse lichen communities in North America.

◄ Greater diversity   Less diversity ►

Lichens form the dominant vegetation over eight percent of earth's terrestrial surface. Worldwide there are more than 14,000 species. In North America we can find 3,600 species. Here in the North Woods, there are more than 700 species. Our local hot spot is Isle Royale, in Lake Superior, with over 600 species. Diversity decreases as you move south and east within our range to as few as 100 species in the furthest south and east section in central Michigan.

The northern Great Lakes area is a member of four larger North American lichen distribution patterns—the boreal element, the pan-temperate element, the east-temperate element and the Appalachian-Great Lakes element. Growing conditions atop mountains in Georgia are similar to some conditions here. Many of the lichens found in Maine grow here too. The North Woods is rich in lichen biodiversity.

Lichens can be found on the ground, on rocks and on trees. The surface for specific lichens can be very limited—to Jack Pine bark, for example—or extremely variable. The surface, or *substrate*, in most cases provides nothing more than a place to attach and grow. Important features of the substrate include texture, moisture retention and chemistry.

Gravestones may host a whole community of lichens. In this case a Firedot species (*Caloplaca*).

Ground Substrates include soil, sand, mosses and decomposing downed logs. Ground lichens produce *hyphae* that bind soil particles and act as soil stabilizers. They also make contributions to soil fertility in the form of organic matter and usable nitrogen. Light colored lichen crusts reflect heat and allow soils to remain cool and moist. Not only do lichens bind soil particles, they also trap dust and provide growth sites for other vegetation to germinate.

Ground substrate

Rock Substrates include cliffs, talus, boulders, pebbles, concrete and shingles. Look among the "mosses" up on your roof— you will see more lichens than you ever expected! Lichens are the primary invaders and colonizers of bare rock growing among rock crystals or under the rock surface. The most highly specialized endolithic lichens occur in Antarctica. Some lichens penetrate the rock matrix several millimeters in granite and up to 16mm in limestone.

Rock substrate

Tree Substrates include conifers and deciduous trees. As bark ages, it often undergoes a change in texture and chemistry. Young maples have a smooth bark; older maple bark is softer and more absorbent with cracks that ooze alkaline, nitrogenous compounds. The older trees often have a greater diversity of lichens. Elm and poplar bark are low in acidity, stable and fairly absorbent. Oak, hickory

tree substrate

Lichens can grow on a variety of substrates. We have organized the book on this basis.

and linden have hard, rough, acidic bark and host very different species. Beech and other trees with smooth, living, green bark are home to yet another community of lichens.

Lichen communities on conifers are often very different than deciduous tree communities. Conifer bark is rich in organic resins and gums and is acidic. The canopy is dense—little light penetrates to the trunk and stems below. Spruce and fir branches sloping downward allow rain to fall to the forest floor rather than running down the trunk. Some lichens are adapted for growth on the branch tips where rainwater runs.

Just as lichens play a role in succession as primary colonizers on bare rock or soils, there are noticeable patterns of micro-succession in some lichen communities. For further description, please turn to the three main substrate sections—ground, rock and tree.

The symbiosis

Symbiosis, a cooperative relationship, is central to the study of lichens. The cow—cornerstone of America's food industry—is a walking lab of symbiosis. Their mammoth four-part stomach is a vat of bacteria, without which the cow would be unable to digest its cud. Chew on that.

Lichens are formed by a partnership between fungi and algae, or cyanobacteria

Lichen

Bacteria (Monera)

Fungi (Fungi)

Algae (Protista)

Plants (Plantae)

Animals (Animalia)

Kingdoms

We are a walking lab of symbiosis too. In fact, consider all eukaryotic cells—those with a nucleus—found in all animals, plants and fungi. Besides the nucleus, eukaryotic cells contain many, many other structures. Mitochondrion—one of these structures—extracts useful energy out of food. Scientists have evidence that, about 2.5 to 3 billion years ago, mitochondria first developed as endosymbiotic bacteria, living inside the cells of another organism. Chloroplasts, the green photosynthetic structures in plant cells, developed from unicellular algae.

Foresters accept that healthy woodlands are a complex web of interacting, symbiotic relationships. It's more than just trees. Spruce trees provide the proper texture for draping Beard Lichens. Beard Lichens provide nesting materials for Northern Parulas. These warblers weave a cavity into the hanging mass. They then gobble up thousands and thousands of black flies. Black flies serve in the transfer of nutrients from streambeds back onto the land via the guts of their predators. Bird droppings and lichens boost soil fertility—especially through additions of nitrogen—leading to robust spruce trees.

The North Woods may look homogeneous from the air but it is actually a complex web of interacting, symbiotic relationships.

Biologist Lynn Margulis, famous for her work on symbiosis and her work with James Lovelock on the Gaia Theory, considers the Darwinian view of evolution based on competition and "survival of the fittest" incomplete at best. She contends evolution is driven by cooperation, interaction and mutual dependence. "Life did not take over the globe by combat, but by networking." As with lichens, organisms that cooperate with others of their own or different species are often more successful than those that do not.

Anatomy of a Lichen

A lichen is typically a layered agglomeration of **fungi** with **algae** and/or **cyanobacteria**. There's one problem in that "typical" isn't really typical. The only certain thing in lichens is the fungal host. That is precisely why taxonomists name and categorize the lichen by the mycobiont, or fungal component. It may more properly be described as lichenized fungi. The fungus is most often a member of the large group of **Ascomycetes**, which includes cup fungi, lobster fungi and morels. Very few arise from **Basidiomycetes**, or the more noticeable mushrooms with a cap and stalk. More than 20 percent of all fungi worldwide are lichenized and these fungi will not grow in nature in an un-lichenized state.

Cross-section of a typical lichen

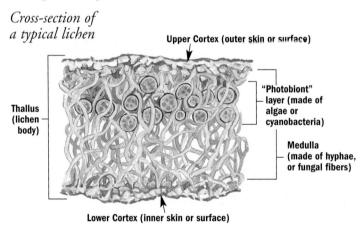

Upper Cortex (outer skin or surface)

Thallus (lichen body)

"Photobiont" layer (made of algae or cyanobacteria)

Medulla (made of hyphae, or fungal fibers)

Lower Cortex (inner skin or surface)

Fungi provide a protective cover for the **photobiont**, or photosynthetic partner. Photobionts are commonly members of the unicellular algae in *Trebouxia* and the filamentous algae in *Trentepohlia*, although only about two to three percent of the photobionts have been identified to species. It is difficult to identify the photobiont to species in part because its appearance is substantially altered when part of the sym-

Trebouxia (unicellular green algae)

biosis. *Trebouxia* is extremely common in lichens, but is not known to occur outside the lichen symbiosis. In contrast, there are many forms of free-living Trentepohlia. You have seen it as the reddish wash on the bright white bark of paper birch.

Some species form partnerships with nitrogen-fixing cyanobacteria of the groups **Nostoc** or *Stigonema*. Cyanobacteria produce the dark colors in many of the dark gray, brown or black lichens such as *Collema*, *Leptogium* and *Peltigera*. Some *Peltigera* house both unicellular algae and cyanobacteria. Even more complex, some lichens contain more than two different species of photobionts or even undergo a change of photobionts during a lifetime.

Nostoc
(nitrogen-fixing
cyanobacteria)

Often, distinct layers form in the lichen *thallus*, or body. Below the upper cortex of fungal tissue is a loosely associated blend of mycobiont and photobiont called the *medulla*. Some lichens have a distinct lower *cortex* while others are simply attached at the medulla.

Lichens are most commonly divided into three growth forms: *crustose*, *foliose* and *fruticose*.

Crustose lichens look like spray paint on the substrate. The lower surface (or medulla) blends directly into the substrate to which it adheres.

Foliose lichens look like leafy growths divided by lobes. The lower surface is distinct and often differently colored from the upper cortex.

Crustose lichens

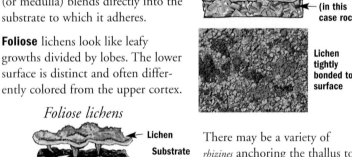

← Lichen

Substrate
← (in this
case rock)

Lichen
tightly
bonded to
surface

Foliose lichens

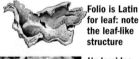

← Lichen

Substrate
← (in this
case rock)

Lichen
attached at
occasional
points with
stem-like
rhizines

Folio is Latin
for leaf: note
the leaf-like
structure

Undersides
often dark
or even
black

There may be a variety of *rhizines* anchoring the thallus to the substrate.

Fruticose lichens are literally bushy or shrubby growths. Some branches are erect while others may be tufted or draping. Although extremely variable, in cross-section we can find all the parts. Perhaps most unique among fruticose lichens

Fruticose lichens

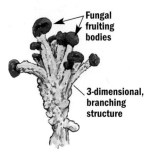

Fungal fruiting bodies

3-dimensional, branching structure

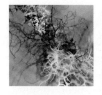

Three forms of fruticose lichens. All could be described as "bushy" or "shrubby." They can be found on all three common substrates.

are the podetia, which are the distinct stalks common to the Pixie Cups (*Cladonia*).

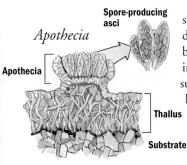

Apothecia

Spore-producing asci

Apothecia

Thallus

Substrate

You will also notice a variety of surface structures. *Apothecia* are the disk or cup-shaped structures formed by the lichen fungus. Spores develop in these sexual structures and presumably land on a suitable photobiont as they grow into lichen. This is all in theory, mind you, since nobody has ever seen it happen in nature. Most likely, either a fragment of healthy lichen or a special asexual structure (*soredia* or *isidia*) are physically detached and land on an appropriate substrate. Soredia and isidia are both bundles of photobiont cells covered with fungal cells. The symbiosis is wrapped in a ready-to-grow package. *Soredia* are surface granules that erupt from the medulla and can be easily brushed off. *Isidia* differ in that they are small growths of the upper cortex and have a shiny surface, in contrast to the dull soredia, which lacks a cortex.

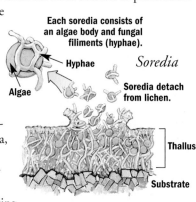

Each soredia consists of an algae body and fungal filaments (hyphae).

Hyphae

Algae

Soredia

Soredia detach from lichen.

Thallus

Substrate

Certainly there are many other structures and some of them are limited to specific groups. A working knowledge of the structures above will serve most of your identification purposes.

Physiology of a lichen

In this tight little package, the lichen has almost all it needs to survive and even thrive. Nutrients and moisture are provided almost exclusively from the atmosphere. They are truly nature's alchemists turning pure air into something more valuable than gold or platinum—they turn air into life. As with many organisms, nitrogen is a limiting factor and some lichens are able to receive all the nitrogen they need from cyanobacteria, which can fix atmospheric nitrogen into usable compounds.

The primary limiting factors for growth are proper substrate, clean air, moisture, sunlight and warmth. Clean air is important really to all organisms. Lichens, however, have no filtering mechanism and so they absorb any and all pollutants. They also have no mechanism to rid pollutants from their system, thus becoming extremely effective bioaccumulators.

The thallus shape is adapted to maximize surface area exposed to moisture and light. When dry, the thallus tends to be opaque protecting the delicate algae below the surface. Once wetted, the translucent thallus allows the sun's radiation to penetrate the cortex providing energy for photosynthesis. Alternating wet and dry periods appear to be important for lichen growth. Too much moisture reduces gas exchange, while being dry for too long will obviously impact growth and survival. Rain, snowmelt, dew and even humidity as low as 60 percent provide the moisture. Liquid water is necessary for cyanobacteria to thrive. Lichens are well adapted for the dry periods. Some Rock Tripe (*Umbilicaria*) can survive as much as 62 weeks without moisture.

Lichens can change appearance dramatically depending on if they are dry or wet. This is Fringed Wrinkle Lichen (*Tuckermanopsis americana*).

The sun provides energy for the photobiont to manufacture carbohydrates from carbon dioxide and other nutrients. With the proper amount of moisture and sunlight, all a lichen needs is a bit of warmth for growth to occur. Summer temperatures may actually be too hot. Many lichens grow best in the cooler periods of spring, fall and even winter. Some lichens continue photosynthesizing in below freezing temperatures. Most growth occurs in spring and fall when temperatures are cool and humidity is high.

In general, lichens are considered extremophiles. Many can survive extreme environments—even conditions of excessive radiation and temperatures that would kill most other organisms in moments. In order to test the possibility of a lichen surviving an interplanetary journey, in June 2005 the European Space Agency took a specimen of Elegant Sunburst Lichen (*Xanthoria elegans*) into space. After being exposed directly to all the perils of space for 14.6 days, it was returned to earth for testing. There was a full rate of survival and an unchanged ability to photosynthesize.

Lichens grow slowly. The Pelt Lichens (*Peltigera*) may grow as fast as 20mm per year while Yellow Map Lichen (*Rhizocarpon*) may grow only 0.09mm per year. The very common Greenshield Lichen (*Flavoparmelia caperata*) will grow 5mm per year. Reindeer lichens (*Cladina*) will live 30 to 50 years and the slow growing Yellow Map Lichens can survive for 4,500 years or more. What you see outside your backdoor today will likely be there with little noticeable change year after year.

Biochemistry

Although many people run screaming when biochemistry is mentioned, you will find it well worth the effort to become somewhat familiar with the chemistry of lichens. As an adaptation for life in marginal habitats, lichens produce unique acids, pigments and other chemicals to control light exposure, repel herbivores, kill attacking microbes and discourage competition from other organisms. Over 700 different secondary metabolites have been identified.

Usnic acid, which produces the light greenish-yellow color in the thallus of Beard Lichens (*Usnea*), is an effective antibiotic being studied for potential human uses. Atranorin absorbs harmful UV light and re-emits the energy as fluorescence usable in photosynthesis. Pigments, such as the bright yellow vulpinic acid and the bright orange parietin, provide a sunscreen to protect the delicate photobiont from damaging UV light. Some pigments serve to regulate temperatures and increase photosynthetic potential.

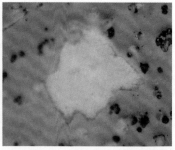 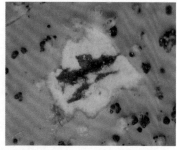

Punctelia rudecta (**Rough Speckled Shield Lichen**) under a microscope. A positive C-Test (right): A drop of reagent on the medulla (cortex scraped away) turns it red. It would be described as "medulla is C+ red (lecanoric acid)" in the *Chemistry* section of the species account.

Slow Growers

After 35 years

Each year Greenshield may grow radially by as much as 5mm. We've shown this actual size.

After 25 years

[By contrast Yellow Map Lichen at this size would be over 1,200 years old!]

After 15 years

After 10 years

Original size (5 years old)

Many chemicals, including fumarprotocetraric acid, are bitter and repel or deter herbivores. Some reduce the growth of potentially competing plants or other lichens. Depsones and depsidones chemically combine with rock minerals to create metal complexes and make the rock more soluble thus speeding the weathering process, although it still takes centuries to create soil.

While the chemistry provides an adaptive advantage to the lichen, knowledge of unique chemistry can also aid in the identification of certain species. William Nylander found in 1866 that the presence of certain chemicals could be determined with color tests. These color tests are used in the identification of many species. Simply apply a drop of the reagent on the thallus, exposed medulla (by scraping away part of the cortex or cutting a cross-section) or apothecia. You may want to use a hand-lens or stereoscope to be certain of your observation. A positive test will result in a color change, while nothing happens in a negative test beyond the slight color change due to wetting.

The primary tests include the K test, the C test, the KC test and the PD test. Potassium hydroxide, caustic lye, for the K test can be obtained as dry sticks from chemical supply companies or you can simply use Liquid Plumber directly from the container. If you purchase the dry sticks you will need to dissolve some small pieces in water to make a ten percent solution. Household bleach can be used for the C test — originally calcium chlorite. The KC test is nothing more than a combination test. First apply K, then C. A pinch of para-phenylenediamine (PD) dissolved in 5 to 10 ml of ethyl alcohol is a useful test for the serious lichenologist. It can only be purchased in large quantities from chemical supply companies and must be handled with care — it will permanently stain anything it touches and is a possible carcinogen.

If you can gain access to a small UV or black light, the UV test is simple and fun. Some lichens fluoresce white, blue or orange. Bright white is a sign of squamatic acid, alectoronic acid, divaricatic acid, evernic acid or perlatolic acid, for example. Rhizocarpic acid fluoresces orange.

We've used Greenshield Lichen (*Flavoparmelia caperata*) as our example. This is a foliose lichen that commonly grows on tree bark.

Lichen Looking & Collecting

Unlike birds, butterflies or many other organisms, there are no special times of year to observe lichens. The only limiting factor may be accessibility. Snow cover will hide the ground lichens; spring snowmelt or summer black flies may make wetlands difficult to explore; and a fear of heights will prohibit exploration of cliff faces and the tops of trees. Other than that, lichens are accessible and relatively unchanged any time of the year.

You can even study lichens in winter!

Making collections

Enjoy lichens in their natural habitat. Although professional lichenologists insist on collections for positive identification in the lab and for scientific purposes, few of us will ever have the need to collect lichens. Leave them right where they grow best. You should only justify collecting lichens if there is a valid scientific or educational intent. It is important to consider the damage of collecting versus the potential benefits of having the specimens.

Close-up photography or sketching will help produce tangible memories of your experience. Program your digital camera to the macro setting and purchase a sturdy tripod to improve the clarity of your pictures. Natural lighting produces the best colors. Avoid the harsh mid-day light or any direct sunlight.

Lichens make fascinating macro photography subjects.

You'll enjoy your close-up photos best if you take pictures in the early morning or late afternoon or if you can find diffused light under a tree canopy, for example. There are several sources for learning more about close-up nature photography [See Appendix A: Titles of Interest]. If you don't have a camera or just want to spend more time observing the lichens, there is nothing better than field sketching with pen or pencil, color or black and white.

Should you decide to make a collection, the following steps will help to assure that the specimen is valuable and the collecting site incurs little damage. Obtain permission from the landowner before making any collection. Collect quality specimens with all the parts including reproductive structures. If the species appears rare in the area or if you have knowledge that the species is threatened in any way, collect only a portion of the specimen if you find it necessary to collect at all. Collect in areas out of site from trails and other high-use areas. Scars on tree bark, rock or the ground will all heal over time…if you are careful to keep the scar small. Better yet, look on the ground among the leaf litter to find specimens that have fallen. This way you will be able to avoid the scars altogether.

Use a small knife for collections from bark; a small chisel for collections on rock. In both cases, be sure to get as much of the complete lichen as possible. Carry small paper bags into the field. Lunch bags will do fine. After collecting, place the specimen into a paper bag and compress the bag just enough to reduce damage in transport. You may find it handy to take notes in a dedicated notebook or simply write on the paper bag. What should you note? Substrate, location (a GPS unit would certainly be handy), habitat, date, ecological notes about the location, anything else of interest and the name of the species.

Advanced identification

When you return home, you will be thankful for all the notes. If you wish to identify the lichen to species, access to detailed scientific manuals, identification chemicals and a microscope is invaluable. With over 700 species to choose from, it can be a challenging process.

Lichenologist Dr. Clifford Wetmore collecting lichen specimens.

Refer to the resources in the back of this guide. At 795 pages and a hefty 8 pounds 9 ounces, *Lichens of North America* is no field guide, but it is an awesome resource. You should consider purchasing it. I have also found Wetmore's *Keys to the Lichens of Minnesota* invaluable. It is available for free from the Minnesota Herbarium website. You may also find it helpful to get a list of possible species from a site near your study area. *NPLichen: A Database of Lichens in the U.S. National Parks* is a great web source of species lists from all over the United States. Much of the advanced identification will require the use of chemicals (see "Biochemistry," page 13, for more detail). Purchase tiny dropper bottles with screw cap lids or re-use well cleaned dropper bottles that you might find being used with various pharmaceuticals —like saline solution. Any of these will produce a drop much larger than is necessary and, in some instances, too large. Professionals use very thin glass pipettes to direct an extremely small amount to a very specific area. Directing drops with toothpicks or cotton swabs may reduce the mess.

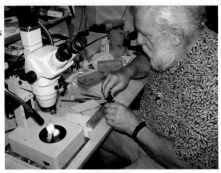
Lichenologist Dr. Theodore Esslinger runs a chemical test on a lichen sample to aid in identification.

What chemicals will you need? The C test is household bleach. The K test is Liquid Plumber. The PD test is paraphenylenedi- amine—you won't find it in your local grocery or hardware store. Contact the botany department of a local college or a DNR

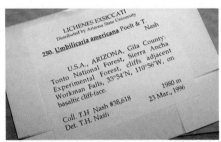
Properly labeled specimen packets are a great research aid for current and future lichenologists.

botanist to learn more. This chemical is really only necessary for truly advanced studies. Finally, a handheld UV or black light is a helpful and fun test. This test is best done in complete darkness in a lab. For more fun, try it outdoors on a moonless night. Since UV light is damaging to skin, be sure to follow the lamp's safety instructions.

A dissecting microscope can be a very useful tool. At minimum you will need a 10x hand lens. As you will notice in the species accounts, many of the measurements are in fractions of millimeters. A small ruler is a must. Then you will also find a razor blade or small X-Acto knife handy when directed to observe aspects of the medulla.

Preserving your collection

Professional herbariums preserve their specimens in packets stored in controlled rooms or cabinets. If you have access, great! If not, you can store your specimens in envelopes, boxes or even the paper bag used for the original collection. Most important—you will want the samples to be accessible, undamaged and well documented. Fortunately, as long as they are kept dry, lichens need no special care and should last in fine condition for decades.

Strict protocols exist for data collection and preservation in formal herbariums. If you wish to preserve at that level, you will be best served to learn from somebody directly from an herbarium. Contact the botany department of a local college or a DNR botanist to learn more. From this point forward we will assume that you will be less formal.

Let's start with the documentation. Following the species name, rewrite all the information clearly on a label that will stay with the specimen. Write your name too — future lichenologists (both amateur and professional) will be glad to know who made the collection. Professionals store their samples in special hand-folded envelopes after the lichens have been pressed. This is to conserve space. When your herbarium begins to take up more space than a closet shelf, you can consider changing methods. Until then, I would suggest that you use small boxes with lids—jewelry boxes, small gift boxes, shoe boxes with dividers or you can even make small boxes by re-using and folding heavy calendar paper. It's easy and fun.

How to use this Field Guide

Order

Lichens are organized first by substrate (ground, rock and tree), then within each substrate group by growth form (crustose, foliose and fruticose) and finally alphabetically by genus. When exploring a rock outcrop, for example, turn to the rock section to page through the many lichens common on this substrate. Once you have isolated a unique lichen and identified its growth form (foliose perhaps), you can further narrow your search to (in this case) 15 species in photos with an additional four similar species described in the text. At this point you can page through the photos to match color, texture and unique surface structures. Read the species text for further details. With experience in the field using this guide, you will gradually learn to identify lichens to genus with a great degree of success.

Lichen Names

Like other organisms, lichens have both common names and scientific names. The common names are English names that most amateurs use. Some of them were only recently invented for the purposes of publishing *Lichens of North America* in 2001. As you cross-reference between other lichen resources, common names are relatively unhelpful. Scientific or Latin names are the spoken word of lichenologists. Since Latin names are in flux, this field guide uses those names also used in *Lichens of North America*. For the most recent names and their synonyms, visit the American Bryological and Lichenological Society's website and look for "A Cumulative Checklist…," which is updated regularly.

Photos

I chose to use close-up photos that also depict the substrate with portions of other lichens likely growing alongside the species. Where appropriate, extreme close-ups are also included to display unique features such as attachment or unique surface features. Photo credits are listed in Appendix C.

Size

Size is difficult to display in the photo without compromising image quality or including too many distractions. It is important to read the text below to get a sense of the true size and scale of the specimen in the field. You will find it handy to take a small metric ruler with you into the field.

Chemistry

Positive identification of lichens often requires chemical testing. If you find the need to identify at the species level, it is best to collect an appropriate specimen and take it back home for further testing. Read the sections on Biochemistry and Advanced Identification for details.

Substrate and Habitat

The most common substrates and habitats are listed clearly below the photo. Your best bet to find the species will be under these conditions—but not exclusively. Some species have very narrow or specific needs while others can vary widely.

Nature Notes

Nature notes are fascinating bits of natural history, unique uses or detailed descriptions of structures that provide a more complete understanding of that species. Population trends, ecology, naming history and other historical accounts are also included.

Species Text

Description includes the best distinguishing characteristics with as little technical jargon as possible. *Thallus* details include color, shape, measurements and unique features. *Apothecia* details, such as color, abundance and size, are included where appropriate. *Chemistry* is included for those seeking an advanced identification. Under *Similar Species*, you will find detailed information regarding differences of species included in other descriptions elsewhere in the book. Also included in this section are similar species not photographed, but relatively common in our area.

Glossary

Check out the glossary for easy to understand meanings for some tricky terms.

Titles of Interest

These books may be of interest to you as you develop a passion for lichens. Appendix A.

Lichen Groups and Websites

Once you get hooked on lichens, you will want to access more information. This section provides some valuable groups, websites and journals to begin developing your expertise. Appendix B.

Habitats where this lichen typically occurs.

The main photo is a diagnostic image of that species. Sometimes a close up showing more detail can be found at the bottom of the page.

Lichens of the North Woods

Orange Rock Posy *Rhizoplaca chrysoleuca*

rocks

Grows on exposed granitic rock.

Description: Foliose pale yellowish-green to dull yellow gray lobes with abundant, pale pink to dark orange disks.

Thallus: Pale yellowish-green to dull yellow gray upper surface with pale brown lower surface attached by a central holdfast.

Apothecia: Abundant pale pink to dark orange disks 2-7mm diameter.

Chemistry: Cortex KC+ yellow-orange (usnic acid)

Similar Species: Granite-speck Rim Lichen (*Lecanora polytropa*) is also common on exposed granite. Although they share substrates and have similar thallus and apothecial colors, *Lecanora polytropa* apothecia are only 0.3-0.8mm diameter.

Nature Notes:
Ever been called a "tree hugger" or "posie sniffer?" Go for it! Sniff the Orange Rock-posy. It doesn't smell like anything, but when you get close enough to be a posy sniffer, you'll no doubt see many other lichens and details unobserved by that crowd of people laughing behind your back.

foliose

FOLIOSE TYPE   **75**

Upper color tab describes the substrate where the lichen is most commonly found (ground, rock or trees).

Nature Notes **are natural history tidbits about that species.**

Lower color tab is where you'll find the growth form of this lichen (crustose, foliose or fruticose).

Growth form is listed on the lower right hand page (Most common substrate is found on the lower left hand page).

Quick Color Tabs make identification easy

trees	rocks	ground

Substrate tabs quickly allow you to flip to the correct section of the book.

fruticose	foliose	crustose

Growth form tabs further organize the lichens within the substrate sections.

Ground Substrate

Terricolous lichens are those species that are most common to ground substrates. The ground substrates include soil, sand, mosses and decomposing downed logs. Look closely at the disturbed soil lifted by roots of tipped over trees, along eroded trailsides and logging roads and in old fields. The sandy and gravelly soils around gravel pits or under spruce, pine and fir canopies provide unique lichen habitats.

Mossy ground, especially on disturbed soils below talus slopes or in pushouts left from road building, can be home to many species including *Peltigera*. Finally, decomposing downed logs, stumps or the occasional wooden fence rail can be a lichen chaos with so many intermixed species of *Cladonia* that it's hard to discern one from the other.

Biological soil crusts (often referred to as cryptogamic, cryptobiotic or microphytic crusts) are a dominant feature in arid and semi-arid landscapes. These crusts are a complex assortment of lichens with mosses, liverworts, cyanobacteria, algae, fungi and bacteria growing in the uppermost layers of the soil. Soil crusts act as soil stabilizers. As well, they hold moisture and provide nutrients such as carbon and nitrogen for vascular plants just becoming established in the harsh environment. Current research suggests that worldwide these soil crusts play a significant role in carbon sequestration. This soil feature dominates large areas of North America, North Africa, Asia and Australia. In our era of global warming, protection of healthy soil crusts is not only ecologically sound, it may also be economically sound as a viable way to reduce atmospheric carbon. Companies, indeed countries, could offset carbon dioxide emissions and meet responsibilities under the Kyoto Protocol by protecting biological soil crusts.

Some common lichens to look for:

Crustose — Mottled Disk Lichen and Candy Lichen.

Foliose — Freckled Pelt and Dog Lichen.

Fruticose — Reindeer Lichen, Pixie Cups, British Soldiers, Dragon Horn, Smooth Horn Lichen.

Crustose Type

24 Brown Beret Lichen (*Baeomyces rufus*)
25 Candy Lichen (*Icmadophila ericetorum*)
26 Greenpea Mushroom Lichen (*Omphalina umbellifera*)
27 Mottled Disk Lichen (*Trapeliopsis granulosa*)

Foliose Type

28 Sea Storm Lichen (*Cetrelia olivetorum*)
29 Common Freckled Pelt (*Peltigera apthosa*)
30 Ruffled Freckled Pelt (*Peltigera leucophlebia*)
31 Concentric Pelt (*Peltigera elisabethae*)
32 Peppered Pelt (*Peltigera evansiana*)
33 Many-fruited Pelt (*Peltigera polydactylon*)
34 Alternating Dog Lichen (*Peltigera didactyla*)
35 Field Dog Lichen (*Peltigera rufescens*)

Fruticose Type

36 Iceland Lichen (*Cetraria islandica*)
37 Star-tipped Reindeer Lichen (*Cladina stellaris*)
38 Green Reindeer Lichen (*Cladina mitis*)
39 Split-peg Lichen (*Cladonia cariosa*)
40 Powdered Funnel Lichen (*Cladonia cenotea*)
41 Mealy Pixie Cup (*Cladonia chlorophaea*)
42 Common Powderhorn (*Cladonia coniocraea*)
43 Lipstick Powderhorn (*Cladonia macilenta*)
44 British Soldiers (*Cladonia cristatella*)
45 Red-fruited Pixie Cup (*Cladonia pleurota*)
46 Trumpet Lichen (*Cladonia fimbriata*)
47 Smooth Horn Lichen (*Cladonia gracilis*)
48 Crazy Scale Lichen (*Cladonia turgida*)
49 Sieve Lichen (*Cladonia multiformis*)
50 Felt Horn Lichen (*Cladonia phyllophora*)
51 Wand Lichen (*Cladonia rei*)
52 Dragon Horn (*Cladonia squamosa*)
53 Easter Foam (*Stereocaulon paschale*)

Brown Beret Lichen   *Baeomyces rufus*

ground

Most often found on soil or shaded rock and occasionally on wood or the bark of roots.

Nature Notes:

Baeomyces literally means small fungus.

The tiny stalks look much like miniature toadstools.

crustose

Although it is the most common Beret Lichen in North America, the size and growth habits make this lichen a treasure to find.

Description: Crustose pale green to gray green surface with short fruticose stalks topped by a dull brown cap.

Thallus: Pale green to gray green rough and warty surface with angular patches.

Apothecia: 1-2mm tall stalks bearing dull brown caps (<2mm diameter) at the top.

Chemistry: Thallus PD+ orange and K+ deep yellow (stictic and norstictic acids).

Similar Species: It is quite unlikely that you will mistake this for any other lichen although it does look a bit like a very tiny *Cladonia*.

Candy Lichen *Icmadophila ericetorum*

ground

Grows among mosses, on well-rotted wood or in peat.

Description: Crustose pale green to bluish green surface with scattered abundant pink disks.

Thallus: Pale green to bluish green thick granular surface.

Apothecia: Abundant pink, white or rose colored disks 1.5-4mm in diameter constricted at the base or with a short stalk.

Chemistry: Apothecia and thallus PD+ orange, K+ deep yellow and UV+ white (thamnolic and perlatolic acids).

Similar Species: This is the only species of *Icmadophila* found in North America. The colorful green and pink lichen is unmistakable.

Nature Notes:

Occasionally, the names of organisms help us to better understand their preferences or life histories.

Icmadophila translated from Greek means moisture loving; *ericetorum* comes from the Greek meaning of the Heath or Ericaceae— plants including Leatherleaf (*Chamaedaphne*), Labrador Tea (*Ledum*) and blueberry (*Vaccinium*).

Look for this lichen while picking blueberries or along the edges of your favorite bog.

crustose

Greenpea Mushroom Lichen *Omphalina umbellifera*

ground

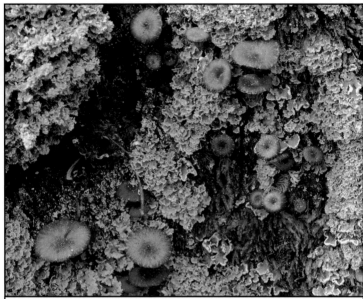

Grows on well-rotted stumps and logs or in shaded mossy soils.

crustose

Nature Notes:

So is it a lichen or is it not? Many lichenologists don't consider this a lichen because it falls within the group of fungus called Basidiomycetes. Only three lichen genera have a basidiomycete as the mycobiont—*Multiclavula, Dictyonema* and *Omphalina*.

Each of the green granules on the thallus surface is actually a tiny fungal envelope packed with hundreds of green algal cells. The granules, once dispersed, are then able to produce a new lichen body.

Description: Crustose bright green surface with seasonally produced orange, waxy mushrooms.

Thallus: Bright green granular to globular surface.

Mushroom: A pale yellow to bright orange mushroom with smooth stems and waxy gills stands 4cm tall.

Chemistry: There is no lichen chemistry.

Similar Species: Without the distinct orange mushrooms, this lichen could be mistaken for any number of sterile *Cladonia* or ground crusts.

Mottled Disk Lichen   *Trapeliopsis granulosa*

Grows on acid soil, peat or rotting wood.

Description: Crustose pale gray to greenish-white thick granular to patchy surface with distinct black dots.

Thallus: Pale gray to greenish-white thick granular to patchy surface.

Apothecia: Pale brown to blackish gray convex disks 0.4-1.5mm in diameter.

Chemistry: Thallus C+ pink (gyrophoric acid).

Similar Species: Board Lichen (*Trapeliopsis flexuosa*) is a similar steel-gray species with flat apothecia growing predominantly on wood, especially fences and boards in full sun.

Nature Notes:

Because this species is an important colonizer of bare soil, forest managers in Quebec have spread it over recently burned forestland to prevent soil erosion.

These lichens produce hyphae that bind soil particles and also make contributions to soil fertility. Additionally, by changing the dominant color of the surrounding area from the soil's dark brown to a pale gray of the lichen, light and heat are reflected allowing the soil to remain both cool and moist.

Sea Storm Lichen *Cetrelia olivetorum*

Grows on bark or mossy rocks in the forest.

Nature Notes:

Look closely at the wavy lobes of this lichen. It's easy to imagine a storm tossed sea covered by foamy green waves.

The pits on the surface are pseudocyphellae and they may be white or a variety of colors. Pseudocyphellae serve as vents for gas diffusion into and out of the lichen.

Description: Foliose greenish gray broad undulating lobes with a tan to black lower surface.

Thallus: Greenish gray with broad, undulating lobes (5-20mm wide), powdery or granular margins, lower surface black in the middle shifting to brown at the edges and tiny pits on upper surface mostly <.3mm diameter.

Apothecia: Extremely rare.

Chemistry: Medulla C+ red (olivetoric acid).

Similar Species: Chicita's Sea Storm Lichen (*Cetrelia chicitae*) has larger pits on the surface and contains alectoronic acid (medulla UV+ blue-white and C-). This species is named after Chicita Culberson, a leading lichen chemist and professor of botany at Duke. Her husband, Bill, was also a lichenologist at Duke. Together the Culbersons helped advance the field of lichenology in many ways. Now that's symbiosis!

Common Freckled Pelt *Peltigera apthosa*

ground

Grows on mossy ground, rocks or tree bases.

Description: Foliose gray-green to brown (green when wet) wide lobes with brown spots on the upper surface. The lower surface is black turning white at the margins.

Thallus: Gray-green to brown when dry (and grass-green when wet) lobes up to 40mm wide with grayish brown gall-like growths 0.5-2mm diameter. The lower surface is black to brown turning white at margins.

Apothecia: Red-brown disks 7-15mm diameter on lobe margins with a uniform surface on the back.

Chemistry: All reactions are negative. Tenuiorin, gyrophoric acid and triterpenes are present.

Similar Species: Ruffled Freckled Pelt (*Peltigera leucophlebia*) has blacker more distinct veins on the lower surface, ruffled margins and a patchy appearance on the back of the apothecia.

Nature Notes:

The brown gall-like growths on the lobes are called cephalodia, and are actually patches of a species of cyanobacteria called *Nostoc*, which converts atmospheric nitrogen into usable nitrates. As a result, this lichen is an important source of nitrogen to the ecosystems in which they grow.

foliose

wet

Ruffled Freckled Pelt   *Peltigera leucophlebia*

ground

Grows on moist, mossy soil, logs or rocks.

Nature Notes:

foliose

Some species of *Peltigera* can grow extremely fast—for lichens, that is; more than 20mm per year. Considering that they are covered with snow for much of the year, that is impressive. Moist habitats, nitrogen-fixing *Nostoc* and a green algae photobiont (Coccomyxa) in the thallus make fast growth possible.

When the thallus is wetted it becomes somewhat transparent and the green algae becomes obvious. Until wet, the thallus is opaque and serves as a protective cover to protect the dry algae.

Description: Foliose gray or brown (green when wet) wide wavy edged lobes. Lower surface white with distinct dark veins and tufted rhizines.

Thallus: Gray or brown when dry and grass-green when wet lobes up to 30mm wide with wavy margins and scattered dark gray cephalodia on surface. The lower surface is white with distinct brown veins and tufted rhizines.

Apothecia: Red brown saddle shaped fruiting bodies with scattered patches of green on lower surface.

Chemistry: All reactions are negative. Tenuiorin, gyrophoric acid and triterpines are present.

Similar Species: Common Freckled Pelt (*Peltigera apthosa*) has distinct brownish growths on the surface and the apothecia have a uniform surface on the back.

Concentric Pelt *Peltigera elisabethae*

Grows on soil or mossy rock faces in forests.

Description: Foliose gray to chestnut brown shiny lobes with a mostly black lower surface.

Thallus: Gray to chestnut brown shiny lobes 10-20mm wide with lower surface mostly black.

Apothecia: None

Chemistry: All reactions are negative. Contains tenuiorin, gyrophoric acid and triterpenes.

Similar Species: Peppered Pelt (*Peltigera evansiana*) has a dull, rough surface.

Nature Notes:

Darker lichens like Concentric Pelt contain cyanobacteria in the medulla. It is the same cyanobacteria, *Nostoc*, common in *Collema*, *Leptogium* and *Peltigera*. *Nostoc* also can be found growing naturally outside the lichen thallus among mosses and soil.

Nitrogen is not part of the earth's crust, but it is found in the atmosphere. Nitrate and ammonia are inorganic forms of nitrogen readily processed by organisms. *Nostoc* is able to take atmospheric nitrogen and convert it to usable forms for the lichen.

Peppered Pelt   *Peltigera evansiana*

ground

Grows on soil in open or forested areas.

foliose

Nature Notes:

North America's 28 species of *Peltigera* are fairly well represented in our region. Considering that they are often covered with snow, have a growing season averaging 90 to 120 days and lichen growth rates are naturally slow, it is really quite impressive that they are able to be so successful.

Description: Foliose pale to dark brown lobes with dull, rough surface slightly downturned at margins. The lower surface is pale at edges and darker in the center.

Thallus: Pale to dark brown lobes 7-25mm wide with dull, rough surface and slightly downturned at the margins. The lower surface is pale at edges and darker in the center with unbranched rhizines.

Apothecia: None.

Chemistry: All reactions are negative. Contains no lichen substances.

Similar Species: Concentric Pelt (*Peltigera elisabethae*) has a shinier surface and also lacks apothecia.

Many-fruited Pelt *Peltigera polydactylon*

ground

Grows on soil, moss or rock in forests.

Description: Foliose shiny brown narrow lobes with abundant red-brown saddle-shaped projections on upturned lobes.

Thallus: Shiny brown lobes 7-10mm wide with lower surface pale at edges becoming dark brown in center and brown rhizines 2-4mm.

Apothecia: Abundant red-brown saddle-shaped bodies on upturned lobes.

Chemistry: All reactions are negative. Contains tenuiorin, gyrophoric acid and triterpenes.

Similar Species: Concentric Pelt (*Peltigera elisabethae*) has a similar thallus but lacks the apothecia on the margins.

Nature Notes:

As the name implies, there are many fruiting bodies — apothecia — on the lobe margins. These apothecia are the sexual reproductive structures for the fungal component or mycobiont. In theory, tiny spores are released from the apothecia and fall to the ground to grow with free-living Nostoc. This process has actually never been witnessed in any natural setting. It's accepted that vegetative reproduction must also be quite common.

foliose

Alternating Dog Lichen *Peltigera didactyla*

ground

Grows on disturbed mossy soil or among mossy rocks.

Nature Notes:

In the absence of sexual reproductive structures —apothecia—this lichen has many round granular patches called soralia (clusters of soredia which contain a bit of the photosynthetic organism wrapped in a web of fungal tissue). When they land on a suitable substrate, the soredia can begin to grow into a new lichen thallus.

foliose

soralia

Description: Foliose brownish gray small lobes with round patches of blue-gray. Lower surface is very pale with whitish rhizines.

Thallus: Brownish-gray lobes up to 10mm wide with round patches of blue-gray granular soredia. The lower surface is very pale with whitish rhizines.

Apothecia: Red-brown, saddle-shaped fruiting bodies on the margins are less commonly seen.

Chemistry: No lichen substances.

Similar Species: There are really no similar species. The small, rounded lobes with gray patches of soredia are quite distinct.

Field Dog Lichen   *Peltigera rufescens*

ground

Grows on soil, fields or sandy areas in full sun. Especially common on roadsides or in open fields.

Description: Foliose brown to brownish gray lobes with a fuzzy surface and strongly upturned margins. The lower surface is white to brownish with tufted rhizines.

Thallus: Brown to brownish-gray lobes mostly 10-25mm wide with a fuzzy surface and margins strongly upturned. The lower surface is white to brownish with tufted or fibrous rhizines.

Apothecia: Reddish-brown saddle-shaped projections from margins of lobes.

Chemistry: No lichen substances.

Similar Species: Dog Lichen (*Peltigera canina*) has larger lobes 10-25mm wide with slightly down-curled margins.

Nature Notes:

Dog lichens are named for the erect apothecia that look like dog ears.

The Doctrine of Signatures gave rise to "Dr. Mead's Pulvus Antilyssus." Simply mix a half-ounce of powdered *Peltigera* with two drachmas of black pepper and a half-pint of warm milk. Taken on four consecutive days, the medicine was claimed to cure rabies.

foliose

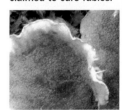

Iceland Lichen *Cetraria islandica*

Grows in heath and on forest floors, especially in pine stands in sandy soils.

Nature Notes:

Very few lichens have actually been used as a food source for humans. In times of need, northern Europeans ground Iceland Lichen and added it to breads and porridges. A common name in Norway is "Bread Moss."

Other names include Icelandic Moss and Consumption Moss.

Today you can find it in herbal medicines used to treat a variety of ailments including sore throat, harsh coughs and tuberculosis.

Description: Fruticose reddish-brown flattened, occasionally rolled up lobes with many white dots on the lower surfaces.

Thallus: Reddish-brown flattened lobes1-10mm wide that may be flat to rolled-up with many white dots on the lower surface.

Apothecia: Resembles the thallus color and texture.

Chemistry: Medulla PD+ red (fumarprotectraric, protolichesterinic and lichesterinic acids).

Similar Species: This is a very unique species. It is actually an erect foliose lichen, but looks very much like a broad fruticose lichen. Nothing else growing on the ground in our area looks like it.

Star-tipped Reindeer Lichen   *Cladina stellaris*

ground

Grows on the ground and in heath.

Description: Fruticose pale yellowish-green tufts forming neatly pruned rounded heads.

Thallus: Pale yellowish-green tufts forming rounded heads 20-40mm across made of many-branching stems with tips terminating in star-like clusters.

Apothecia: None.

Chemistry: Thallus KC+ gold and UV+ blue-white (usnic and perlatolic acid).

Similar Species: Often growing among other *Cladina* and *Cladonia*. Seperate from Green Reindeer Lichen (*Cladonia mitis*) by Star-tipped's distinct ball-like rounded heads.

Nature Notes:

This is the lichen preferred as a winter food source for caribou and reindeer herds. Caribou, on the Slate Islands, Ontario (Lake Superior), have eaten much of the available lichens from the ground and from the trees up as far as they can reach. They utilize ground lichens in fall and spring then tree lichens in winter. Caribou have bacteria in their gut that can process lichen materials into usable nutrients.

Some Inuit people eat partially digested lichen directly from the stomach of freshly killed caribou.

fruticose

Green Reindeer Lichen   *Cladina mitis*

Grows over thin soils, rock, heath, mosses and grassy areas in full sun.

Nature Notes:

It is very common to see three or four *Cladina* species intermixed in a single clump.

Reindeer Lichens play a critical role in the survival of boreal and arctic ecosystems by maintaining soil moisture and temperature. Even when the top is dry and crusty, dig your hand down beneath the cushion and you will find it moist and flexible.

Cladina inhibits the growth of other lichens by its chemicals.

The ground cover in some forests can form an almost continuous mat of Reindeer Lichen with spruce and fir trees intermixed.

Description: Fruticose pale yellowish-gray to yellow-green tufts composed of many-branching stems.

Thallus: Pale yellowish-gray tufts of tree-like branching stems with tips curved in all directions and perhaps slightly browned.

Apothecia: None.

Chemistry: Thallus KC+ yellow containing usnic and rangiformic acid.

Similar Species: Gray Reindeer Lichen (*Cladina rangiferina*) lacks any of the greenish pigments and has all its tips pointed in the same directions.

Split-peg Lichen   *Cladonia cariosa*

ground

Grows directly on the soil.

Description: Fruticose gray to gray-green stalks rising from scale-like surface of the same color and topped with large chocolate-brown caps.

Thallus: Gray to gray-green stalks up to 30mm tall arising from scale-like surface of patches 1-3 by 0.5-2mm.

Apothecia: Chocolate-brown caps atop the stalks.

Chemistry: There are two chemical races—one has fumarprotocetraric acid and atranorin (PD+ red and K+ yellow) and the other has only atranorin (K+ yellow).

Similar Species: Wand Lichen (*Cladonia rei*) has a distinct greenish tinge to the stalks.

Nature Notes:

More than 700 secondary substances have been identified in lichens. They serve the lichens in so many different ways. Atranorin, for example, absorbs damaging rays of UV light and re-emits them as a fluorescence in a wavelength that can be utilized for photosynthesis. Atranorin both protects the lichen and makes unusable energy usable.

fruticose

Powdered Funnel Lichen   *Cladonia cenotea*

Grows on earth or wood usually in the shade.

Nature Notes:

This lichen is common in boreal forests. Find this species and you are very likely in a forest defined by its geology and climate. Look around. Do you see mosses, spruce and fir? With a growing season less than 90 days and snow cover for most of the remainder of the year, this is a tough place to grow.

In this author's humble opinion, spruce, fir, black flies and lichens rule the boreal forest.

Description: Fruticose greenish-gray powdery somewhat browned stalks open at the top to a hollow interior.

Thallus: Greenish-gray powdery stalks (10-70mm tall) browned and open at the top to a hollow interior.

Apothecia: Uncommon. Brown if present.

Chemistry: UV+ Blue-white (squamatic acid).

Similar Species: Dragon Horn (*Cladonia squamosa*) has a much coarser surface.

ground

fruticose

Mealy Pixie Cup *Cladonia chlorophaea*

ground

Grows on wood, bark, rock or soil in full sun or partial shade.

Description: Fruticose pale green, gray green or brownish goblet-shaped cups arising from an abundantly patchy surface of the same color.

Thallus: Pale green, gray green or brownish goblets 2-6mm wide rising up to 35mm tall from a patchy surface.

Apothecia: Large brown caps formed on short stalks arising from the cup margins.

Chemistry: PD+ red (fumarprotocetraric acid).

Similar Species: Several species are included in the *chlorophaea* group. They all look very similar. Pebbled Pixie Cup (*Cladonia pyxidata*) has rounded patches on the edge of the cups. Gray's Pixie Cup (*Cladonia grayi*) contains grayanic acid — UV+ blue-white. Trumpet Lichen (*Cladonia fimbriata*) is more finely dusted and narrowly trumpet shaped.

Nature Notes:

Fourteen chemotypes are known in this complex throughout North America. What's a chemotype? Many lichens can only be identified by their unique chemistry. Researchers at Duke University studied this group of lichens and found that — although they were mostly unidentifiable visually — the taxonomics could be sorted out by the presence or absence of compounds.

fruticose

Common Powderhorn *Cladonia coniocraea*

ground

Grows on soil, tree bases and wood in shade.

Nature Notes:

Until the early part of the 20th century, lichenologists tasted lichens to determine the presence or absence of the bitter chemical fumarprotocetraric acid. This aided in identification of specific lichens such as Common Powderhorn.

In 1939, Yasuhiko Asahina (1880-1975) and his students in Japan developed the use of paraphenylenediamine (PD) as a color reagent. PD turns red in the presence of the acid. Phew, no more taste tests.

fruticose

Description: Fruticose gray-green or olive stalks with a granular surface arising from rounded greenish lobes.

Thallus: Gray green or olive granular unbranched stalks10-25mm tall rising from rounded greenish lobes 6mm broad.

Apothecia: Brown, rare.

Chemistry: Thallus PD+ red (fumarprotocetraric acid).

Similar Species: Bighorn Lichen (*Cladonia cornuta*) is browner and usually in the full sun.

Lipstick Powderhorn *Cladonia macilenta*

Grows on old wood or soil and occasionally on rock.

Description: Fruticose grayish or greenish slender, unbranched stalks arising from finely scaled surface and topped with a blunt red tip.

Thallus: Grayish or greenish slender, unbranched stalks 10-30mm tall arising from a finely scaled (<2mm broad) surface.

Apothecia: Bright red, blunt tips on the top of stalks.

Chemistry: Two chemical races—one PD+ orange (thamnolic acid) and the other KC+ yellow to orange (barbatic acid).

Similar Species: British Soldiers (*Cladonia cristatella*) has much more branching at the tips.

Nature Notes:

As if it were not already difficult enough to identify lichens to species, Lipstick Powderhorn (like many other lichens) has a distinct chemistry, which allows some to describe it even further down to a chemical race.

Of the two chemical races, the thamnolic acid race is more commonly found on rocks.

ground

fruticose

British Soldiers   *Cladonia cristatella*

ground

Grows on wood, soil and tree bases.

Nature Notes:

This is perhaps the most commonly know lichen. Why? It is pollution-tolerant growing readily where large population centers occur, it is very colorful and it earned a common name long ago.

Most lichens have only recently earned common names as a way to make them more accessible to those intimidated by Latin. Many of the common names in this book were only recently developed for the book, *Lichens of North America* published in 2001.

Description: Fruticose greenish gray to yellowish gray stalks topped with a bright red caps and arising from an abundantly patchy surface.

Thallus: Greenish gray to yellowish gray stalks less than 25mm tall arising from a very patchy surface.

Apothecia: Bright crimson red caps.

Chemistry: Thallus KC+ orange containing usnic, barbatic and didymic acids.

Similar Species: Red-fruited Pixie Cup (*Cladonia pleurota*) has the distinct red apothecia, but also has distinct cups whereas the British Soldiers lacks cups.

fruticose

Red-fruited Pixie Cup *Cladonia pleurota*

ground

Grows on wood, bark or soil.

Description: Fruticose pale yellowish-green cups rising from scaly surface. The cups have bright red caps on the margins.

Thallus: Pale yellowish-green granular stalks with cups 6-25mm tall rising from a scaly surface.

Apothecia: Bright red proliferations on the margins of the cups.

Chemistry: Thallus KC+ gold containing usnic acid and zeorin.

Similar Species: British Soldiers (*Cladonia cristatella*) do not have cups. Mealy Pixie Cup (*Cladonia chlorophaea*) and related species do not have the bright red apothecia.

Nature Notes:

Splash cups, found in Pixie Cups, provide a means of dispersing reproductive materials of the lichen and thus proliferating the species.

The red apothecia are reproductive structures for the fungus. Look closely at the surface to see granular soredia— bundles of algae wrapped in a fungal web. Since the likelihood that fungal spores will land on a suitable algae and then form a lichen symbiosis is statistically small, soredia most likely contribute to the majority of reproductive successes.

fruticose

Trumpet Lichen *Cladonia fimbriata*

Grows on soil or rotting wood in full sun or partial shade.

Nature Notes:

Of the 128 species of *Cladonia* in North America, not all have the unique goblet or trumpet-shaped stalks, but when present they certainly are distinct.

These splash cups aid in the reproductive efforts of the lichen. As rainwater splashes into the cup, vegetative structures or spores from apothecia (often situated on the lip of the cup) are forcefully ejected from the lichen to a nearby spot hopefully to grow into a new lichen body.

Description: Fruticose gray-green to green or olive-gray goblet or trumpet shaped stalks arising from a scale-like surface.

Thallus: Gray-green to green or olive gray trumpet shaped stalks 10-20mm tall rising from a scale-like surface of the same color.

Apothecia: Brown.

Chemistry: Thallus PD+ red (fumarprotocetraric acid).

Similar Species: Mealy Pixie Cup (*Cladonia chlorophaea*) has wider cups that are more proliferating.

Smooth Horn Lichen   *Cladonia gracilis*

ground

Grows on exposed soil or wood.

Description: Fruticose greenish to olive or brown stalks arising from a scaly surface and topped with well-developed cups producing brown caps on the margins.

Thallus: Greenish to olive or brown stalks 2-5cm tall rising from a scaly surface topped with well-developed cups.

Apothecia: Brown caps produced on the margins of cups.

Chemistry: Thallus PD+ red (fumarprotocetraric acid).

Similar Species: Felt Horn Lichen (*Cladonia phyllophora*) can resemble this species but they have rougher cup margins and a duller surface. A subspecies of *Cladonia gracilis*, common in temperate areas, lacks cups and looks a bit like Common Powderhorn (*Cladonia coniocraea*) which grows 3-8cm tall.

Nature Notes:

These species can become quite browned in the direct sun, which is likely an adaptation to protect the algae from harmful radiation.

Ultraviolet light, in particular, can be very damaging to organisms of all sorts. Consider all the varieties of sunglass that we have at our disposal to protect us from UV-A and UV-B light.

Ozone depletion is a threat to life on earth, allowing more UV-B to enter our space. Some lichens produce chemicals for protection.

fruticose

Crazy Scale Lichen *Cladonia turgida*

ground

Grows in shaded forest soils often among mosses.

Nature Notes:

Technically, the growth form is not fruticose, but squamulose. The wavy growths among the *Cladonia* are referred to as squamules. Most identification guides—including this one—lump this growth form into either foliose or fruticose.

This is an arctic-alpine species meaning that we are at the southern reaches of its range at this elevation. Follow the Appalachians down to Georgia and you will find it growing on mountain tops with other common North Woods plants like blueberry, spruce and feathermosses.

fruticose

Description: Fruticose dark greenish-gray or olive smooth branching lobes.

Thallus: Dark greenish-gray or olive smooth lobes 10mm across and 20mm long branching with wide-open axils but no cups.

Apothecia: None.

Chemistry: Medulla PD+ red and K+ pale yellow (atranorin and fumarprotocetraric acid).

Similar Species: Some clumps may be similar to Thorn Lichen (*Cladonia uncialis*) which grows on rock and is usually much more tufted and branching.

Sieve Lichen *Cladonia multiformis*

ground

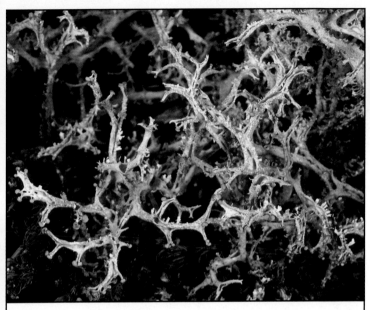

Grows on thin mineral soil in sun to partial shade.

Description: Fruticose grayish green to brownish stalks with extremely variable shapes.

Thallus: Grayish-green to brownish stalks up to 45mm tall.

Apothecia: Brown caps.

Chemistry: Thallus PD+ red (fumarprotocetraric acid).

Similar Species: Felt Horn Lichen (*Cladonia phyllophora*) usually has a duller appearance and the bases of the stalks are often spotted with black. Smooth Horn Lichen (*Cladonia gracilis*) has cups that are always closed.

Nature Notes:

As the name *multiformis* implies, this lichen can have many forms. It is often difficult to distinguish it from other species. The PD chemical test may be necessary for positive identification.

fruticose

Felt Horn Lichen   *Cladonia phyllophora*

ground

Grows on soil in the open or in partial shade.

Nature Notes:

While some secondary substances like usnic acid and atranorin serve as a sunscreen for the algae, fumarprotocetraric acid most likely serves as a deterrent to potential herbivores. The acid has a distinct bitterness once actually used by lichenologists as an identification characteristic. The bitterness most likely encourages some herbivores to seek out other food.

fruticose

Description: Fruticose dull olive to grayish green stalks with gradually broadening cups having puffy margins.

Thallus: Dull olive to grayish green stalks 10-60mm tall with gradually broadening cups 1-4mm across.

Apothecia: Brown arising from margins of the cups.

Chemistry: Thallus PD+ red (fumarprotocetraric acid).

Similar Species: This species is often confused with either Smooth Horn Lichen (*Cladonia gracilis*) or Sieve Lichen (*Cladonia multiformis*) except that neither of these species has a puffy soft surface or a spotted base.

Wand Lichen   *Cladonia rei*

ground

Grows on soil or wood in the open.

Description: Fruticose gray green to olive stalks with dark brown proliferations on the cup margins arising out of a finely granular surface.

Thallus: Gray green to olive stalks <20mm tall arising out of a finely granular surface.

Apothecia: Dark brown proliferations on the cup margins.

Chemistry: Podetia PD+ red (homosekikaic acid).

Similar Species: Split-peg Lichen (*Cladonia cariosa*) has a much coarser surface and is much less likely to have a green tinge.

Nature Notes:

This often grows as a pioneer species in old-field succession along-side British Soldiers (*Cladonia cristatella*) and other species of *Cladonia*.

Although it is some-times difficult to identify the various species growing so closely among each other, if you page through the photos of *Cladonia* included in this field guide, you will likely be able to identify many different species on a single downed log, among mosses or on poor soil.

fruticose

Dragon Horn   *Cladonia squamosa*

ground

Grows on soil or logs in deep shade.

Nature Notes:

This very common lichen inhabits moist and shaded areas. Look at the bases of trees among mosses for its typical habitat.

The squamatic acid fluoresces bluish-white under UV light. You won't see the reaction unless it is dark. You can take a sample inside or, better yet, find a portable black light and wander the woods at night looking for lichens and other organisms that fluoresce under UV light.

Description: Fruticose pale grayish green abundantly scaly stalks arising from a very scaly surface of the same color.

Thallus: Pale grayish-green abundantly scaly and somewhat branched stalks (up to 40-50mm tall) arising from a very scaly surface of the same color.

Apothecia: Brown caps, occasionally seen.

Chemistry: UV+ blue-white (squamatic acid).

Similar Species: Powdered Funnel Lichen (*Cladonia cenotea*) has in-rolled cup margins.

fruticose

Easter Foam   *Stereocaulon paschale*

Growing on soil.

Description: Fruticose gray to white stalks with a very coarse, granular surface and woody base.

Thallus: Gray to white somewhat erect mat of smoothish stalks 2-6cm tall with blackish and roughened outgrowths in clusters.

Apothecia: Convex and brownish black at the end of the stems.

Chemistry: Cortex K+ yellow containing lobaric acid and atranorin.

Similar Species: Woolly Foam (*Stereocaulon tomentosum*) grows in loose mats on the ground and has stalks with puffy white covering of fine fuzz and is PD+ orange (sticitc acid). Other *Stereocaulon* grow on rock.

Nature Notes:

This lichen can grow so dense as a ground cover that the soil temperature and moisture are affected. The ecology of spruce trees in the boreal forest are uniquely dependent upon *Stereocaulon* and *Cladina*.

Stereocaulon comes from the greek words *stereo* meaning "solid" and *caulon* meaning "stalk."

As with many lichens, the photosynthetic partner can vary from one individual to another. Although Easter Foam always has a species of cyanobacteria, it can either be *Nostoc* or *Stigonema*.

ground

fruticose

Rock Substrate

Saxicolous lichens are those species that are most common to rock substrates. Rock substrates include cliffs, talus, boulders, pebbles, concrete and shingles. Siliceous rocks—granites, schists and other igneous rocks with high quartz content—dominate the North Wood's geology and are commonly home to Rock Tripe (*Umbilicaria*) and Rockshield (*Xanthoparmelia*). North facing cliffs tend to be cooler and wetter than south facing cliffs—look for larger Rock Tripe on the north faces and Golden Moonglow Lichens (*Dimelaena oreina*) on drier, hotter faces.

Rock communities on lakeshores are great places to explore. The rock closest to the water line (and ice in winter) is often quite bare looking although it is home to hardy, resilient crustose lichens. Just above this zone but still within reach of spray from waves, are some of the most diverse lichen communities you'll find. Cliff faces and bird perch sites along Lake Superior's shore are often adorned with very distinct orange Elegant Sunburst Lichens (*Xanthoria elegans*).

Talus, or loose angular rock at the base of a cliff, can be difficult to traverse with many ankle-twisting holes. It is worth the effort, though, to see the equally unpredictable patterns and textures of Reindeer Lichens (*Cladina*) and other species. Boulders and pebbles may not look very promising at first, but upon closer examination you'll begin to see the differences between the crystalline structures of the rock in comparison to the patterns of crustose lichens. Concrete and shingles are also home to many unique crustose species.

Succession of saxicolous communities on bare rock proceeds from a variety of crustose lichens to foliose and then fruticose species.

Some common lichens to look for:

Crustose — Cinder Lichen, Concentric Boulder Lichen, Yellow Map Lichen.

Foliose—Rock Tripe, Rock Shield, Sunburst Lichen.

Fruticose—Reindeer Lichen, Bushy Lichen, Rock Foam.

Crustose Type

56 Dusty Cobblestone Lichen (*Acarospora americana*)
57 Cinder Lichen (*Aspicilia cinerea*)
58 Sulphur Firedot (*Caloplaca flavovirescens*)
59 Granite Firedot (*Caloplaca arenaria*)
60 Common Goldspeck (*Candelariella vitellina*)
61 Golden Moonglow Lichen (*Dimelaena oreina*)
62 Tile Lichen (*Lecidea tesselata*)
63 Rock Disk Lichen (*Lecidella stigmatea*)
64 Zoned Dust Lichen (*Lepraria neglecta*)
65 Concentric Boulder Lichen (*Porpidia crustulata*)
66 Yellow Map Lichen (*Rhizocarpon geographicum*)
67 Single-spored Map Lichen (*Rhizocarpon disporum*)

Foliose Type

68 Concentric Ring Lichen (*Arctoparmelia centrifuga*)
69 Jelly Flakes Lichen (*Collema undulatum*)
70 Brook Stickleback Lichen (*Dermatocarpon luridum*)
71 Leather Lichen (*Dermatocarpon miniatum*)
72 Common Toadskin Lichen (*Lasallia papulosa*)
73 Tattered Jellyskin (*Leptogium lichenoides*)
74 Powdery Kidney Lichen (*Nephroma parile*)
75 Orange Rock Posy (*Rhizoplaca chrysoleuca*)
76 Peppered Rock Tripe (*Umbilicaria deusta*)
77 Smooth Rock Tripe (*Umbilicaria mammulata*)
78 Plated Rock Tripe (*Umbilicaria meuhlenbergia*)
79 Frosted Rock Tripe (*Umbilicaria americana*)
80 Cumberland Rock Shield (*Xanthoparmelia cumberlandia*)
81 Shingled Rock Shield (*Xanthoparmelia somloensis*)
82 Elegant Sunburst Lichen (*Xanthoria elegans*)

Fruticose Type

84 Gray Reindeer Lichen (*Cladina rangiferina*)
85 Quill Lichen (*Cladonia amaurocraea*)
86 Thorn Lichen (*Cladonia uncialis*)
87 Rock Bushy Lichen (*Ramalina intermedia*)
88 Rock Foam (*Stereocaulon saxatile*)

Dusty Cobblestone Lichen *Acarospora americana*

rocks

Grows on granitic rock in full sun.

Nature Notes:

crustose

Succession on rock begins with crustose lichens. Some of the first to establish a saxicolous community include *Acarospora*, *Porpidia*, *Rhizocarpon* and *Lecidea*.

There are 77 species of *Acarospora* in North America all exclusive to rock in full sun.

Description: Crustose dusty brown loosely patchy surface.

Thallus: Dusty brown loosely patchy (0.5-3mm diameter) surface becoming lifted at the edges.

Apothecia: Immersed in the center of each patch.

Chemistry: No positive lichen tests.

Similar Species: Brown Cobblestone Lichen (*Acarospora fuscata*) is cortex C+ red containing gyrophoric acid.

Cinder Lichen   *Aspicilia cinerea*

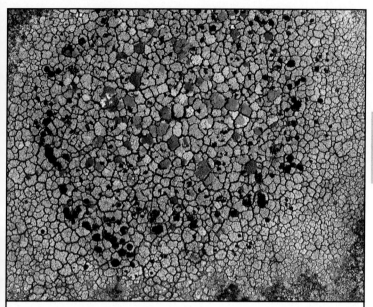

Grows on siliceous rocks in sun.

rocks

Description: Crustose pale to ashy-gray thin to thick surface with black spots level with the surface.

Thallus: Pale to ashy-gray thin to thick continuous surface.

Apothecia: Black disks 0.4-1.2mm diameter level with surface.

Chemistry: Medulla PD+ yellow to orange and K+ yellow to red (norstictic acid).

Similar Species: Blue Cinder Lichen (*Aspicilia caesocinerea*) has a blue-gray thallus and medulla K-.

Nature Notes:

A related species, *Aspicilia esculenta*, grows in Middle Eastern deserts. As it grows, small chunks can be freed from its substrate. It has been used in local bread recipes and some people believe that this may have been the "manna from heaven" that served the Israelites.

crustose

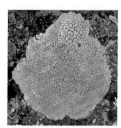

Sulphur Firedot   *Caloplaca flavovirescens*

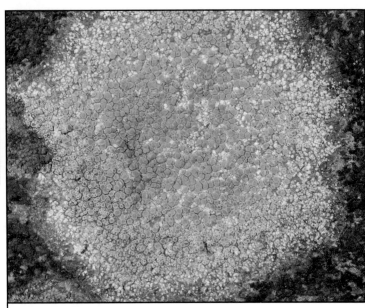

Grows on rocks of all sorts.

rocks

Nature Notes:

With 131 species in North America, *Caloplaca* lichens are very successful. They are so tiny that most people overlook them. Once you take the time to get close to the rock, you'll soon notice how common they are among the rock crystals and other lichens.

crustose

Description: Crustose smooth yellow surface with reddish-orange disks.

Thallus: Smooth yellow surface.

Apothecia: Reddish-orange disks 0.4-0.8mm diameter.

Chemistry: Thallus and apothecia K+ deep purple (anthraquinones).

Similar Species: Common Goldspeck (*Candelariella vitellina*) tends to be more yellow than orange and its thallus is K-.

Granite Firedot   *Caloplaca arenaria*

Grows on siliceous rock in full sun.

rocks

Description: Crustose gray surface occasionally with crowded dark red-orange dots.

Thallus: Gray surface occasionally evident.

Apothecia: Crowded dark red orange disks 0.2-0.5mm diameter.

Chemistry: K+ deep purple (anthraquinones).

Similar Species: Sidewalk Firedot (*Caloplaca feracissima*) is very common on mortar, cement and natural limestone.

Nature Notes:

The Granite Firedot thallus grows within the upper layers of the rock —in and around rock crystals. Some endolithic lichens can grow up to 16mm into the rock matrix. This type of growth erodes the surface of the rock. Lichen chemicals can react with the minerals. Perhaps more effective is the physical erosion caused by the expansion and contraction of water in the lichen cells. Matching the pace of the growth of these lichens themselves, erosion of this sort moves at an extremely slow pace.

crustose

Caloplaca lichens can be quite common on gravestones.

Common Goldspeck   *Candelariella vitellina*

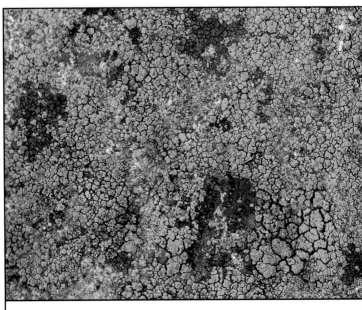

rocks

Grows on granitic rock in full sun.

Nature Notes:

crustose

This is a very common rock lichen that is frequently overlooked. Check especially in and among the more robust foliose lichens.

The chemical, Calycin serves the lichen as a sunscreen, regulating the solar intensity at the algal layer. *Trebouxia*, the most common algae in lichen symbioses, grows best at a relatively low light intensity.

Description: Crustose small yellow cushions.

Thallus: Yellow in very small cushions.

Apothecia: Crowded yellow flat disks 0.5-1.5mm diameter.

Chemistry: UV+ dull, dark orange (calycin).

Similar Species: Powdery Goldspeck (*Candelariella efflorescens*) is an extremely faint and small lichen common on tree bark.

Golden Moonglow Lichen *Dimelaena oreina*

rocks

Grows on sunny siliceous rock mostly on vertical surfaces.

Description: Crustose yellowish surface sometimes blackening at edges with small lobes on the margins and black dots level with surface.

Thallus: Yellowish lobes 0.5-1mm wide and 1-3mm long sometimes blackening at the edges with central patches 0.3-1mm diameter.

Apothecia: Black disks level with the thallus.

Chemistry: Chemical races of medulla include PD+ orange (fumarprotocetraric acid), C+ red (gyrophoric acid) or K+ yellow (norstictic acid).

Similar Species: Some extremely faded individuals may be confused with Cinder Lichen (*Aspicilia cinerea*). Look for the tiny yellowish lobes in *Dimelaena* to eliminate other lichens.

Nature Notes:

Golden Moonglow Lichen is widespread across North America although it is restricted to open habitats such as rock outcrops, cliff faces and glacial erratics in prairie regions.

Lichens play a small role in the erosion of rock surfaces. The release of CO_2 in the presence of H_2O forms H_2CO_3 — a weak acid that can affect some rock minerals.

crustose

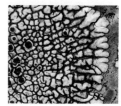

Tile Lichen   *Lecidea tesselata*

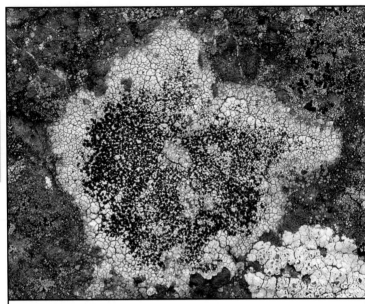

Grows on rock in full sun.

rocks

crustose

Nature Notes:

The Tile Lichens, all 136 species, are strictly rock-dwelling and they grow within the rock matrix. In general, endolithic species such as this have the adaptive advantage of being able to photosynthesize and grow at temperatures hovering around freezing. During brief mid-winter thaws, as snowmelt wets the rock, these lichens are growing.

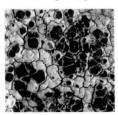

Description: Crustose chalky white to blue-gray surface forming circular patches with sunken black disks.

Thallus: Chalky white to blue-gray surface forming circular patches.

Apothecia: Black disks sunken in thallus.

Chemistry: No positive lichen tests (confluentic acid).

Similar Species: Most of North America's 136 species simply look like black dots. Identification requires examining individual spores under magnification.

Rock Disk Lichen   *Lecidella stigmatea*

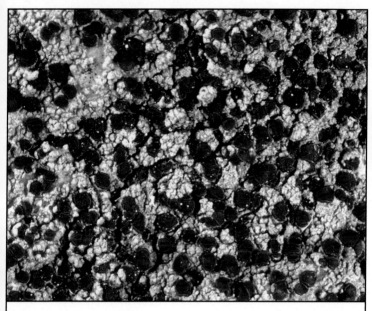

rocks

Grows on rock surfaces.

Description: Crustose dirty gray to yellowish -white surface with flat or convex black disks.

Thallus: Variable dirty gray to yellowish-white surface.

Apothecia: Black flat or convex disks 0.4-1.2mm diameter.

Chemistry: Thallus K+ yellow (zeorin and atranorin).

Similar Species: In the field, it is easy to mistake this lichen with Tile Lichen (*Lecidea tesselata*) or Concentric Boulder Lichen (*Porpidia crustulata*). The K+ yellow thallus is key in the identification.

Nature Notes:

The colorless substance atranorin, found in a variety of lichens, is useful to the lichen as a UV light filter. Both atranorin and stictic acid may cause photocontact dermatitis, in which an allergic reaction to the substance is more intense when the skin is exposed to the lichen substances in combination with sunlight.

crustose

Zoned Dust Lichen *Lepraria neglecta*

rocks

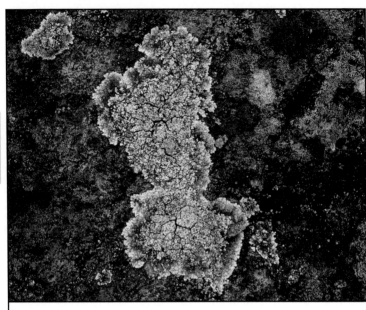

Grows commonly on partially shaded granitic rock.

crustose

Nature Notes:

Dust Lichens are nothing more than a continuous layer of granular soredia. Each of the spherical aggregations of soredia looks like small cotton balls. Unfortunately, the cotton balls won't absorb water — it simply beads up on the surface and is unavailable to the lichen. Dust Lichens most likely obtain all their moisture from humidity in the air.

Description: Crustose blue gray surface forming distinct rings or zones.

Thallus: Blue-gray granular or fuzzy surface in distinct rings.

Apothecia: None.

Chemistry: Thallus PD+ yellow and C+pink (alectorialic acid).

Similar Species: Nothing really looks like it. The granular, fuzzy surface with distinct rings stands alone.

Concentric Boulder Lichen   *Porpidia crustulata*

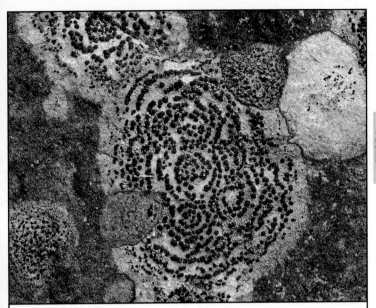

Grows on siliceous rock in full sun or shade.

rocks

Description: Crustose pale greenish-gray thin surface with dark brown disks in concentric patterns.

Thallus: Pale greenish-gray and very thin. The thallus is occasionally oxidized orange.

Apothecia: Numerous dark brown disks 0.3-1.0mm diameter in a concentric pattern.

Chemistry: Lichen tests are unreliable.

Similar Species: Many other crustose species including the Tile Lichens (*Lecidea*) and Map Lichens (*Rhizocarpon*) are superficially similar.

Nature Notes:

Like most of our lichens, the alga in this relationship belongs to the genus *Trebouxia*. This green algae is a unicellular, usually spherical alga containing a large stellate (star-like) chloroplast. Although *Trebouxia* is most widespread and successful as a photobiont in lichens of all sorts, it can be found growing in nature on tree bark.

crustose

Yellow Map Lichen *Rhizocarpon geographicum*

rocks

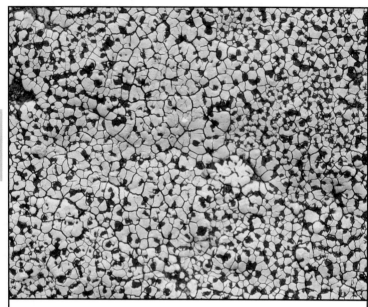

Grows on exposed siliceous rock.

crustose

Nature Notes:

Yellow Map Lichen is the poster child of lichenometry—the use of lichen aging techniques to determine the age of geologic events such as the retreat of glaciers or the sloughing of huge rock surfaces. It is quite common in some areas to find *Rhizocarpon* over 1000 years old. One set of lichen thalli in the Brooks Range, Alaska was found growing at a rate of 0.09mm per year. That organism, at 480mm diameter, is several thousand years old. Lichens over 4500 years old have been reported from Swedish Lapland.

Description: Crustose yellow to yellowish-green shiny surface with black dots tucked in the margins.

Thallus: Yellow to yellowish-green shiny surface.

Apothecia: Black dots tucked within thallus margins.

Chemistry: Cortex UV+ orange (rhizocarpic acid).

Similar Species: Yellow Soot Lichen (*Cyphelium lucidum*) is restricted to pine bark.

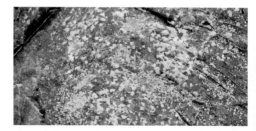

Single-spored Map Lichen *Rhizocarpon disporum*

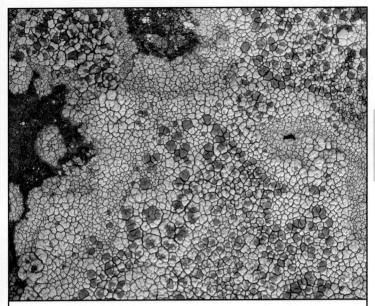

Grows on exposed siliceous rock.

Description: Crustose brownish gray to pale gray surface with black dots.

Thallus: Brownish gray to pale gray surface.

Apothecia: Black disks 0.4-1mm diameter.

Chemistry: No reliable lichen tests.

Similar Species: Boreal Single-spored Map Lichen (*Rhizocarpon grande*) medulla reacts C+ red and K+ yellow.

Nature Notes:

Where is the lichen? The non-yellow Map Lichens look so much like the rock on which they grow, you may have never even noticed them. Yet another reason to find a quiet piece of rocky Lake Superior shoreline and contemplate important things like...lichens.

rocks

crustose

Concentric Ring Lichen   *Arctoparmelia centrifuga*

rocks

Grows on siliceous rock in the open.

Nature Notes:

foliose

Listed as a sensitive species in the Superior National Forest it exists exclusively along the North Shore of Lake Superior in the region covered by this guide.

Because we are at the southernmost edge of its range, global warming will likely reduce populations in the North Woods.

Average growth rates may be 2mm per year. The oldest parts of the ring are often only 30-50 years old. Thallus parts older than 50 years die back and leave bare rock. Rings up to a meter across may be as much as 500 years old.

Description: Foliose greenish-yellow flat lobes with a white lower surface scattered with rhizines.

Thallus: Greenish-yellow flat lobes 1-2mm wide with lower white surface and scattered rhizines. Older individuals form a characteristic donut-shaped ring.

Apothecia: Brown disks are rare.

Chemistry: Cortex K+ yellow, thallus UV+ white and medulla KC+ red (alectoronic acid).

Similar Species: The Rock Shields (*Xanthoparmelia*) have a shiny upper surface and brown or black lower surface.

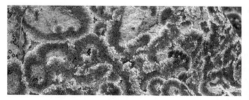

Jelly Flakes Lichen *Collema undulatum*

rocks

Grows on rock.

Description: Foliose dark yellowish-brown to black lobes with distinctly undulating margins.

Thallus: Dark yellowish-brown to black 1-5mm lobes with distinctly undulating margins.

Apothecia: Uncommon flat to convex red-brown disks.

Chemistry: No lichen chemistry. Contains no lichen substances.

Similar Species: Tree Jelly (*Collema subflaccidum*) does not have wavy, undulating margins and grows on mossy trees.

Nature Notes:

Dark lichens almost always have cyanobacteria in the mix. Cyanobacteria, or blue-green algae, have the ability to convert atmospheric nitrogen into a usable form. In harsh rock communities, the presence of cyanobacteria provides an adaptive advantage that makes Jelly Flakes a relatively common lichen in depressions with a regular flow of water.

foliose

Brook Stickleback Lichen *Dermatocarpon luridum*

Common on siliceous rock in and along streams.

rocks

Nature Notes:

When wet, the cortex of the lichen (composed of fungal cells) becomes transparent and makes it possible to see the algal layer. This adaptation insures that the algae are protected by a dark fungal layer in times of drought, but are exposed to the sun when enough moisture is present to sustain photosynthesis. This is perhaps the main adaptive advantage found in many lichens. A variety of specialized pigments are produced in lichens for protecting the algae from intense light while also regulating temperatures within the thallus.

Description: Foliose brownish-gray leathery lobes turning green when wet.

Thallus: Brownish-gray leathery lobes 7-20mm wide turning green when wet (above). Lacks rhizines.

Apothecia: Embedded in thallus appearing as tiny black dots.

Chemistry: No lichen substances.

Similar Species: Leather Lichen's (*Dermatocarpon miniatum*) numerous small lobes grow in a concentration of spherical clumps and does not turn green when wet.

dry

Leather Lichen *Dermatocarpon miniatum*

Common on rock in dry places.

rocks

Description: Foliose gray leathery lobes growing in spherical clumps.

Thallus: Gray leathery lobes often growing as a single spherical clump 15-45mm diameter. Does not turn green when wet.

Apothecia: None.

Chemistry: No lichen substances.

Similar Species: Brook Stickleback (*Dermatocarpon luridum*) grows on wet rock and turns green when wetted.

Nature Notes:

Leather Lichen reproduces exclusively through fragmentation. Lobes occasionally break free of the rock surface and are then lodged in a crack, crevice or depression that provides suitable growing conditions.

foliose

Common Toadskin Lichen *Lasallia papulosa*

Grows on boulders and cliff faces in the sun.

rocks

Nature Notes:

Papillosa comes from the Latin meaning "many pimples." The pimples are an important characteristic not present in the Rock Tripes often found growing alongside Common Toadskin.

The wetted surface reveals the greenish color of the symbiotic algae just below the protective surface. Dribble a little water on it and watch "the toad" come alive.

foliose

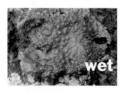

Description: Foliose dark brown lobe with extremely abundant pustules paired with corresponding pits on the lower surface. Attached to rock with a single holdfast.

Thallus: Dark brown, dull surface attached by a central point and sometimes covered with a rusty red dust. The pustules are extremely abundant and correspond with pits on the smooth, pale to medium brown lower surface.

Apothecia: Tiny black dots.

Chemistry: Medulla C+ red (gyrophoric acid) and rusty red dust (if present) K+ purple (anthraquinones).

Similar Species: Rock Tripes (*Umbilicaria*) lack the distinct pustules on the upper surface with corresponding pits on the lower surface.

Tattered Jellyskin *Leptogium lichenoides*

rocks

Grows on mossy rock.

Description: Foliose dark brown jelly like lobes that are quite inconspicuous forming cushions with wrinkled, upright and finely divided edges.

Thallus: Dark brown cushions of wrinkled upright lobes 1-4mm wide with finely divided edges.

Apothecia: Fairly common red brown disks 0.2-0.7mm diameter on the lobe surface.

Chemistry: No lichen substances.

Similar Species: Blue Jellyskin (*Leptogium cyanescens*) has a blue-gray thallus with thin, smooth lobes 2-4mm wide and grows on bark at bases of trees, mossy logs and on mossy shaded rock.

Nature Notes:

When wet, Jellyskins take on a jelly-like appearance — thus the name. Jellyskins, although inconspicuous, are quite common throughout our area.

Leptogium requires a relatively low light intensity to achieve maximum rates of nitrogen fixation. As such, you will find them under a dense forest canopy or more commonly at the bases of trees and on mossy rock.

foliose

wet

Powdery Kidney Lichen   *Nephroma parile*

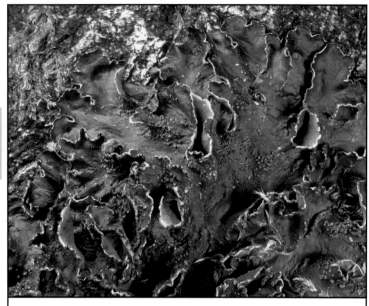

Grows on mossy rock or trees in shaded forests.

Nature Notes:

The "powder" on this lichen's margins is called soredia. Soredia are present as a vegetative reproductive structure. Each of the tiny granules is actually a tiny globe of fungal tissue surrounding viable cells of the blue-green algae, *Nostoc*. As with many other lichens, the dark thallus is a sign of the presence of nitrogen-fixing *Nostoc*.

Description: Foliose chocolate brown lobes with abundant brown to gray granules on margins.

Thallus: Chocolate brown (becoming olive when wet) lobes 4-8mm wide with abundant brown to gray soredia on margins. Lower surface smooth, pale brown.

Apothecia: Rare.

Chemistry: No positive lichen tests. Zeorin in many specimens.

Similar Species: Both Peppered Moon Lichen (*Sticta fuliginosa*) and Yellow Specklebelly (*Pseudocyphellaria crocata*) have a rough lower surface with distinct pits scattered on that lower surface. Powdery Kidney Lichen has a smooth lower surface.

Orange Rock Posy *Rhizoplaca chrysoleuca*

rocks

Grows on exposed granitic rock.

Description: Foliose pale yellowish-green to dull yellow gray lobes with abundant, pale pink to dark orange disks.

Thallus: Pale yellowish-green to dull yellow gray upper surface with pale brown lower surface attached by a central holdfast.

Apothecia: Abundant pale pink to dark orange disks 2-7mm diameter.

Chemistry: Cortex KC+ yellow-orange (usnic acid).

Similar Species: Granite-speck Rim Lichen (*Lecanora polytropa*) is also common on exposed granite. Although they share substrates and have similar thallus and apothecial colors, *Lecanora polytropa* apothecia are only 0.3-0.8mm diameter.

Nature Notes:

Ever been called a "tree hugger" or "posie sniffer?" Go for it! Sniff the Orange Rock-posy. It doesn't smell like anything, but when you get close enough to be a posy sniffer, you'll no doubt see many other lichens and details unobserved by the crowd of people laughing behind your back.

foliose

Peppered Rock Tripe *Umbilicaria deusta*

Grows on exposed boulders and outcrops.

Nature Notes:

Deusta comes from *deustus* (Latin) meaning burned up or charred.

Rock Tripes can withstand long periods of drought—up to 62 weeks in some. That is a great adaptation for pioneer species of talus slopes and rock outcrops. In turn, Rock Tripe lobes provide space to capture dust and seeds for the next organisms in line for succession.

Description: Foliose thin, crowded dark brown to black lobes attached by a central holdfast.

Thallus: Thin, crowded dark brown to black lobes 1-5cm diameter with smooth dark brown to black lower surface. Attached by a central holdfast.

Apothecia: Rare.

Chemistry: Medulla C+ red (gyrophoric acid).

Similar Species: Leather Lichen (*Dermatocarpon miniatum*) is gray as opposed to the dark brown or almost black of Peppered Rock Tripe.

Smooth Rock Tripe *Umbilicaria mammulata*

rocks

Grows on steep rock walls and boulders in forests and sometimes on lakeshores.

Description: Foliose moderately thick reddish-brown large lobes connected to substrate
by a central holdfast. Lower surface is pitch
black with a velvety nap.

Thallus: Reddish-brown to grayish-brown
smooth, thick lobes 4-15cm diameter. Lower
surface pitch black with a velvety nap.

Apothecia: Rare.

Chemistry: Medulla C+ red (gyrophoric
acid).

Similar Species: Plated Rock Tripe
(*Umbilicaria muehlenbergia*) is also brown but
lacks the velvety lower surface and scattered
dark brown spots.

Nature Notes:

Rock Tripes grow from a
center umbilicus or
umbilical cord — hence
the name, *Umbilicaria*.
The fastest growing por-
tion of the lichen is at
the center. The edges
are the first to die back
resulting in the tattered
look.

Gyrophoric acid can be
used to make a natural
purple dye. Grind the
lichen then cover it with
a fairly diluted mix of
ammonia and water in
a sealed jar. Only fill a
third full; let air occupy
the top two thirds of the
jar. Allow it to ferment
until you get the desired
effect. It may take 2 to
6 weeks.

foliose

Plated Rock Tripe   *Umbilicaria meuhlenbergia*

rocks

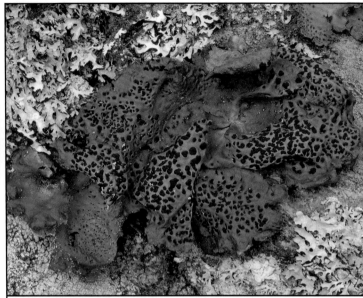

Grows on boulders and steep rock faces in forests and in the open.

Nature Notes:

Muehlenbergia was named in honor of Henry Muhlenberg (1753-1815), a pioneer botanist and Lutheran minister in Pennsylvania. His work focused on sedges, grasses and rushes—not lichens. But famed lichenologist Edward Tuckerman was responsible for his herbarium. That seems to be the only connection between Muhlenberg and lichens.

foliose

The Cree people once used this as a thickening agent in fish broth. It was also used to feed sick people since it did not upset the stomach, which is curious given the inedibility of *Umbilicaria* in general.

Description: Foliose almost shiny dark brown to gray lobes with scattered dark brown spots and a central holdfast. Lower surface pale brown to black with a network of overlapping plates.

Thallus: Dark brown to gray lobes 6-15cm diameter with an almost shiny surface. Lower surface pale brown to black with a network of overlapping scales and a central holdfast.

Apothecia: Common dark brown to black disks 1-4mm diameter usually sunken in depressions.

Chemistry: Medulla KC+ red and C+ red (gyrophoric acid).

Similar Species: Smooth Rock Tripe (*Umbilicaria mammulata*) when young has a velvety nap below, not plates. It can also be superficially mistaken for Common Toadskin (*Lasallia papulosa*) which has distinct pits on the upper and lower surface.

Frosted Rock Tripe   *Umbilicaria americana*

Grows on steep granitic rock faces in partially shaded sites.

rocks

Description: Foliose pale gray thick and stiff lobes with a coarse white dusted upper surface. Lower surface velvety black.

Thallus: Pale gray or brownish-gray lobes 2-7cm diameter with a coarse white dusted upper surface. Lower surface velvety black with a central holdfast and dark, simple rhizines.

Apothecia: Uncommon.

Chemistry: Medulla C+ red (gyrophoric acid).

Similar Species: Arctic Frosted Rock Tripe (*Umbilicaria vellea*) has pale, branched rhizines.

Nature Notes:

Rock tripes have served as survival food for many Arctic explorers. Although these lichens were among the many unique substances eaten by starving adventurers, some preferred to eat their boots before resorting to Rock Tripe. *Umbilicaria* are generally difficult for humans to digest, they have a high acid content, they cause diarrhea and they don't taste so good either. May you never be forced to choose between rock ttripe and your hiking boots.

foliose

Cumberland Rock Shield *Xanthoparmelia cumberlandia*

rocks

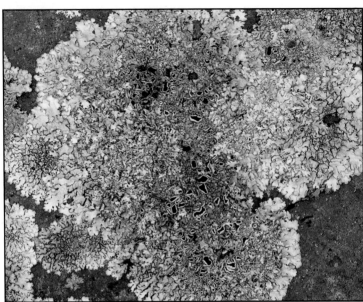

Grows on exposed to somewhat shaded rock outcrops and boulders.

Nature Notes:

Some say size doesn't matter. Apparently they haven't read "*Sexual Fecundity is Correlated to Size in the Lichenized Fungus Xanthoparmelia cumberlandia*" (Not printed in *Cosmopolitan*, by the way). According to the paper, sexual success, or fitness, is indeed determined by size. Lichens with larger apothecia are apparently more successful.

foliose

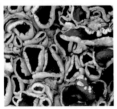

Description: Foliose yellowish green lobes tightly attached to the rock and forming large radiating patches with brown disks crowding the center. Lower surface pale to medium brown.

Thallus: Yellowish-green lobes 1.5-4mm wide tightly attached to the rock often forming large radiating patches up to 12cm diameter. The lower surface is pale to medium brown with unbranched rhizines.

Apothecia: Abundant brown disks 2-8mm diameter often with rolled margins crowding the center of the thallus.

Chemistry: Medulla PD+ orange and K+ yellow (stictic, constictic and norstictic acids).

Similar Species: Shingled Rock Shield (*Xanthoparmelia somloensis*) is more loosely attached to the rock and has salazinic acid (K+ yellow changing rapidly to blood-red).

Shingled Rock Shield   *Xanthoparmelia somloensis*

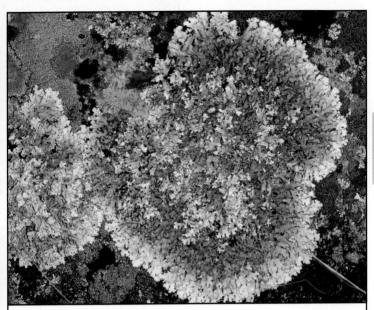

Grows on exposed boulders and outcrops.

rocks

Description: Foliose yellowish green lobes forming radiating patches often darkened gray in the central portions with brownish disks.

Thallus: Yellowish-green lobes .3-2.5mm wide often constricted just behind the tips. The lower surface is pale brown with margins occasionally blackened.

Apothecia: Brown disks 3-7mm diameter common and somewhat raised.

Chemistry: Medulla PD+ yellow and K+ yellow turning rapidly to blood-red (salazinic acid).

Similar Species: Plitt's Rock Shield (*Xanthoparmelia plittii*) has lobes 1-3mm wide that are crowded and overlapping and apothecia are rare. Also this species does not contain salazinic acid.

Nature Notes:

Succession on bare igneous rock in the North Woods usually begins with the crustose lichens *Acarospora, Porpidia, Rhizocarpon* and *Lecidea.*

The Rock Shields (*Xanthoparmelia*) are some of the most common foliose lichens to follow and prepare the surface. The next stages include more foliose lichens including *Phaeophyscia* and *Parmelia. Cladonia* lichens, mosses and grasses dominate the final stage of succession in this lichen community.

foliose

Elegant Sunburst Lichen *Xanthoria elegans*

rocks

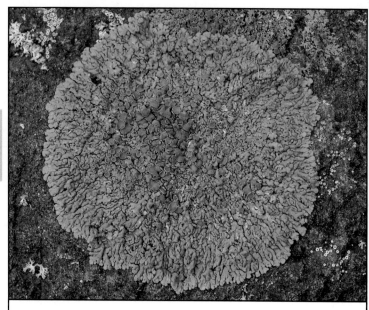

Grows on rock in open sites, and on wood or bone.

Nature Notes:

foliose

Elegant Sunburst Lichen is very common on rocks fertilized by birds and mammals. It's very prominent along the shores of Lake Superior. In contrast, it is surprisingly uncommon in the large inland lakes of Voyageurs N.P. Perhaps this is related to wave action. All Sunburst Lichens (*Xanthoria*) contain parietin which is shown to aid in the absorption of UV-B radiation. As the hole in the ozone layer continues to grow larger over the Antarctic (and it is), some researchers suspect that species with adaptive advantages *(continued on next page)*

Description: Foliose to almost crustose pale yellowish orange to dark reddish orange lobes with a lower white surface and abundant orange disks.

Thallus: Very closely attached pale yellowish orange to dark reddish orange lobes 0.4-1mm wide. Lower surface white without rhizines.

Apothecia: Abundant thallus-colored disks 1-3mm diameter.

Chemistry: Cortex K+ dark red-purple (parietin).

Similar Species: Other *Xanthoria* rarely grow on rock.

rocks

Xanthoria elegans grows on rock and thrives in areas frequented by gulls. Gull droppings provide nitrogen.

The Elegant Sunburst lives up to its name on this rocky stretch of Lake Superior shoreline.

foliose

Nature Notes (cont.)

such as this will thrive as other organisms die off. This lichen is tough. In order to test the possibility of it surviving an interplanetary journey exposed to a harsh space environment, in June 2005 the European Space Agency took a specimen of Elegant Sunburst Lichen into space. After being exposed to all the perils of space for 14.6 days, it was returned to earth for further testing. There was a full rate of survival and an unchanged ability to photosynthesize. Wow! The next question may be, "could the real Martians be lichens?"

Gray Reindeer Lichen *Cladina rangiferina*

Grows over rock or thin soils usually in full sun.

rocks

Nature Notes:

Look at the antler-like branching stems and the name is obvious. Together with other species of *Cladina* and some *Cladonia*, Reindeer Lichen serves as a main winter food for caribou and reindeer.

It takes 15 years to regenerate a pasture heavily browsed by caribou. Boreal woodlands subjected to fire take 80 to 120 years to progress from bare soil to a mature mat of reindeer lichens.

Ojibwa historically made a decoction of this lichen for bathing newborn babies.

Description: Fruticose white to sliver-gray cushions or tufts with branching tree-like main stems.

Thallus: White to silver-gray tufts with somewhat browned bent tips commonly branched in 2s and 3s. The base is gray.

Apothecia: Uncommon.

Chemistry: Tips of branches PD+ red and K+ pale yellow (fumarprotocetraric acid and atranorin).

Similar Species: Black-footed Reindeer Lichen (*Cladina stygia*), common in boggy sites, is very similar in all aspects except for the dark brown to black base. False Reindeer Lichen (*Cladonia wainioi*), one of our 11 protected lichens, is a PD- lichen thriving on bare rock in full sun.

fruticose

Quill Lichen   *Cladonia amaurocraea*

Grows on talus slopes between boulders and on rocky ground.

rocks

Description: Fruticose grayish-green cushions or tufts with irregularly branched stalks having long brownish tapering tips at the margins of cups.

Thallus: Grayish-green often with conspicuous white mottling. Branches 15-100mm high with a smooth surface terminating in narrow cups lined with tapering brownish tips at the margins.

Podecia: Brownish pointed tips arising from cup-like formations on the branches.

Chemistry: No positive tests. Contains usnic and barbatic acids.

Similar Species: Thorn Lichen (*Cladonia uncialis*) is open at the axils.

Nature Notes:

In the North, lichen cover can reach 50-90 percent with an almost continuous mat of *Cladina*, *Stereocaulon* and *Cladonia*. This thick mat of lichens preserves soil moisture and temperature, adds organic matter and traps seeds. Usnic acid inhibits the manufacture of photosynthetic pigments and reduces photosynthesis in plants. This serves the lichen as a way to reduce the growth of potentially competing plants.

Quill Lichen grows as far south as Georgia in the Appalachians.

fruticose

Thorn Lichen   *Cladonia uncialis*

Grows on bare rock and soil or among mosses.

rocks

Nature Notes:

Thorn Lichen, Reindeer Lichen and Star-tipped Reindeer Lichen were the three most caribou-preferred lichens in feeding trials in Quebec. Since lichens make up 90 percent of the winter feed for caribou and reindeer, this is important to know.

Lichens receive all their nutrients from the atmosphere. After the Chernobyl nuclear plant meltdown in the 1980s, radioactive material fall-out found its way from the lichens into the reindeer. Shortly afterward, the Saami culture was devastated by cancer. Their primary meat source is reindeer.

fruticose

Description: Fruticose pale yellow to light greenish-yellow abundantly branched stalks forming cushions or tufts.

Thallus: Pale yellow to light greenish-yellow thin-walled stalks 20-60mm tall with open axils ending in short blunt tips. The surface is often mottled white, yellow or tan with patches of green.

Apothecia: Rare.

Chemistry: UV+ white (usnic acid).

Similar Species: Quill Lichen (*Cladonia amaurocraea*) is closed at the axils.

Rock Bushy Lichen *Ramalina intermedia*

rocks

Grows on rock faces and boulders in forests and along lakes.

Description: Fruticose pale yellow-green bushy body with finely divided flat branches.

Thallus: Pale yellow-green with finely divided flat branches 1-3cm long by 0.2-1mm wide.

Apothecia: Rarely seen.

Chemistry: No positive lichen tests. Contains sekikaic acid.

Similar Species: Other *Ramalina* species grow on trees.

Nature Notes:

Lichen rock communities follow a predictable pattern of succession. Pioneer species include a variety of crustose lichens. After the intermediate foliose species have been established, the climax lichen community dominated by fruticose species can begin to grow. Rock climbers once actively scrubbed cliff faces to rid their climbing routes of lichen. In turn, they unknowingly eliminated many of these old-growth lichen communities. Current North Woods climbing ethics place a high value on protection of healthy cliff ecosystems.

fruticose

Rock Foam   *Stereocaulon saxatile*

Grows directly attached to siliceous rock in full sun.

rocks

Nature Notes:

Although it is not as palatable as the Reindeer Lichens (*Cladina*), Rock Foam becomes a food-source for caribou in times of need.

Pixie Foam (*Stereocaulon pileatum*) often grows on rock with high concentrations of metals like iron or magnesium. In fact, lichens are used worldwide as a prospecting tool. Analysis of the thallus in a lab will reveal the composition of dust in the vicinity. High levels of copper, for example, may indicate the presence of a valuable deposit of copper.

fruticose

Description: Fruticose gray to white branches with a very coarse, granular surface and woody base.

Thallus: Gray to white somewhat erect tight mat (up to 10cm across) of coarse stalks 3-6cm tall. The stem outgrowths are short and flattened.

Apothecia: Convex and black at the end of stems.

Chemistry: Cortex K+ yellow. Contains lobaric acid and atranorin.

Similar Species: Finger-scale Foam (*Stereocaulon dactylophyllum*) has long stems not growing in tufts with long and cylindrical outgrowths from the stalks and the thallus is PD+ orange and K+ yellow. Pixie Foam (*Stereocaulon pileatum*) is a miniature version of the other two that grows about 3mm tall and has no apothecia. Other *Stereocaulon* lichens grow on soil.

Tree Substrate

Corticolous lichens are those species that are most common on trees. While some lichens simply thrive suspended in the air column, others require a very specific substrate, as in American Starburst Lichen (*Imshaugia placorodia*), which will only grow on Jack Pine. Shield Lichens (*Parmelia*) can be found on the trunks of just about any tree. Moosehair (Horsehair) Lichens (*Bryoria*) prefer the tips of Black Spruce branches. You'll also find that spruce and fir branches sloping downward allow rain to fall to the forest floor from the tips of these often-dead branches. Look for Wrinkle Lichens (*Tuckermanopsis*), Crumpled Rag Lichen (*Platismatia tuckermanii*) and Tube Lichens (*Hypogymnia*). Beard Lichens (*Usnea*) are very visible on the dead branches of spruce and fir.

Birch trees, although deciduous, often support communities of lichens expected on coniferous trees such as the Camouflage Lichens (*Melanelia*). Similarly, Cedars, although coniferous, are host to lichens common to deciduous trees including Speckled Shield Lichens (*Punctelia*).

Elm and poplar lichen communities often include Sunburst Lichens (*Xanthoria*), Firedots, (*Caloplaca*) and Rim Lichens (*Lecanora*). Sugar Maple lichen communities vary with the age of the tree stand. Younger maple is often dominated by Oakmoss (*Evernia*), Shield Lichen (*Parmelia*), Greenshield (*Flavoparmelia*) and Goldspeck (*Candelariella*). Older maple bark is softer and more absorbent with cracks that ooze alkaline, nitrogenous compounds. Among the dense mosses, you will find Lungworts (*Lobaria*) and Tree Jelly Lichens (*Collema*).

Succession of corticolous lichen communities begins with foliose and fruticose lichens invading the tree bark and stems first. Climax communities on tree trunks can be quite complex, but often there is a distinct community of crustose lichens.

Some common lichens to look for:

Crustose—Goldspeck, Rim Lichen, Dust Lichen.

Foliose—Greenshield, Shield Lichens, Sunburst Lichens.

Fruticose—Oakmoss, Bushy Lichen, Beard Lichens.

Crustose Type

92   Common Button Lichen   (*Buellia stillingiana*)
93   Common Tree Firedot   (*Caloplaca holocarpa*)
94   Powdery Goldspeck   (*Candelariella efflorescens*)
95   Yellow Soot Lichen   (*Cyphelium lucidum*)
96   Brown-eyed Rim Lichen   (*Lecanora allophana*)
97   Mapledust Lichen   (*Lecanora thysanophora*)
98   Bark Disk Lichen   (*Lecidela euphorea*)
99   Fluffy Dust Lichen   (*Lepraria lobificans*)
100   Bloody Heart Lichen   (*Mycoblastus sanguinarius*)
101   Rosy Saucer Lichen   (*Ochrolechia trochophora*)
102   Bitter Wart Lichen   (*Pertusaria amara*)
103   Whitewash Lichen   (*Phlyctis argena*)

Foliose Type

104   Eastern Candlewax Lichen   (*Ahtiana aurescens*)
105   Candleflame Lichen   (*Candelaria concolor*)
106   Tree Jelly Lichen   (*Collema subflaccidum*)
107   Common Greenshield   (*Flavoparmelia caperata*)
108   Hooded Tube Lichen   (*Hypogymnia physodes*)
109   American Starburst Lichen   (*Imshaugia placorodia*)
110   Lungwort   (*Lobaria pulmonaria*)
111   Smooth Lungwort   (*Lobaria quercizans*)
112   Abraded Camouflage Lichen   (*Melanelia subaurifera*)
113   Spotted Camouflage Lichen   (*Melanelia olivacea*)
114   Treeflute Lichen   (*Menagazzia terrebrata*)
115   Smooth Axil-bristle Lichen   (*Myelochroa galbina*)
116   Bottlebrush Shield Lichen   (*Parmelia squarrosa*)
117   Green Starburst Lichen   (*Parmeliopsis ambigua*)
118   Orange-cored Shadow Lichen   (*Phaeophyscia rubropulchra*)
119   Powder-tipped Shadow Lichen   (*Phaeophyscia adiastola*)
120   Pom-pom Shadow Lichen   (*Phaeophyscia pusillodes*)
121   Hooded Rosette Lichen   (*Physcia adscendens*)
122   Star Rosette Lichen   (*Physcia stellaris*)
123   N. Bottlebrush Frost Lichen   (*Physconia leucoleptes*)
124   Crumpled Rag Lichen   (*Platismatia tuckermanii*)
125   Yellow Specklebelly   (*Pseudocyphellaria crocata*)
126   Rough Speckled Shield Lichen   (*Punctelia rudecta*)
127   Peppered Moon Lichen   (*Sticta fuliginosa*)
128   Fringed Wrinkle Lichen   (*Tuckermanopsis americana*)
129   Powdered Sunshine Lichen   (*Vulpicida pinastri*)
130   Poplar Sunburst Lichen   (*Xanthoria hasseana*)
131   Powdery Sunburst Lichen   (*Xanthoria ulophyllodes*)

Fruticose Type

132   Moosehair Lichen   (*Bryoria trichodes*)
133   Boreal Oakmoss   (*Evernia mesomorpha*)
134   Common Antler Lichen   (*Pseudevernia consocians*)
135   Sinewed Bushy Lichen   (*Ramalina americana*)
136   Bristly Beard Lichen   (*Usnea hirta*)
137   Powdered Beard Lichen   (*Usnea lapponica*)
138   Boreal Beard Lichen   (*Usnea subfloridana*)
139   Methuselah's Beard Lichen   (*Usnea longissima*)
140   Pitted Beard Lichen   (*Usnea cavernosa*)

Common Button Lichen *Buellia stillingiana*

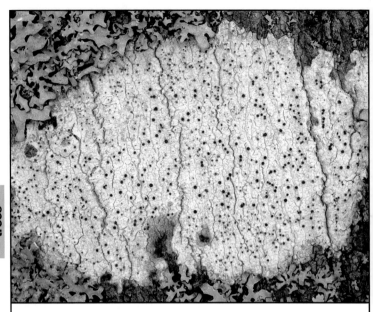

Grows on deciduous trees and conifers.

Nature Notes:

Successional stages of lichen communities on rock progress from crustose lichens, to foliose lichens and then on to fruticose lichens. In contrast, successional stages for lichen communities on tree bark follow an opposite pattern. Many crustose lichens are a sign of an older successional lichen community.

Description: Crustose thin gray surface with flat back disks.

Thallus: Thin, gray surface.

Apothecia: Flat black disks 0.4-0.8mm diameter.

Chemistry: Thallus K+ red (norstictic acid).

Similar Species: Specimens with few apothecia can be confused with Whitewash Lichen (*Phlyctis argena*).

Common Tree Firedot *Caloplaca holocarpa*

Grows on bark and wood of many trees.

trees

Description: Crustose light orange to orangish-yellow disks.

Thallus: Not visible since it develops within the tree bark or wood.

Apothecia: Abundant light orange to orangish-yellow disks 0.5-0.7mm diameter.

Chemistry: Apothecia K+ deep purple (anthraquinones).

Similar Species: Boreal Tree Firedot (*Caloplaca ahtii*) has yellow-orange apothecia 0.1-0.4mm diameter.

Nature Notes:

This Firedot thrives on bark that is low in acidity, stable and fairly absorbent. Elm, maple and aspen provide great substrates for *Caloplaca* and *Lecanora* of all species.

crustose

Powdery Goldspeck *Candelariella efflorescens*

Grows on bark of all kinds.

trees

crustose

Nature Notes:

This is a very common lichen on maple and aspen alike. You can expect to find this species growing where you see *Parmelia*, *Melanelia*, *Physcia* and *Xanthoria*. All of these species form lichen associations on trees referred to as corti-colous communities. Powdery Goldspeck is so tiny that you will need to look very close-ly in some cases to find it growing among the larger foliose lichens.

Description: Crustose yellow surface forming very small round patches.

Thallus: Consists of yellow round, flat patches 0.2mm diameter.

Apothecia: Uncommon.

Chemistry: Thallus UV+ dull, dark orange (calycin).

Similar Species: Common Goldspeck (*Candellaria vitellina*) grows on rock.

Yellow Soot Lichen   *Cyphelium lucidum*

Grows on bark of living conifers.

Description: Crustose bright yellow surface with prominent black disks.

Thallus: Bright yellow.

Apothecia: Prominent black disks 0.5-1mm diameter raised on short stalks.

Chemistry: Contains vulpinic acid.

Similar Species: The only lichen that looks anything like it is Yellow Map Lichen (*Rhizocarpon geographicum*). Luckily for us, *Rhizocarpon* only grows on rock and *Cyphelium* only grows on bark.

Nature Notes:

The yellow pigment is a result of the vulpinic acid, which absorbs longwave UV light. A pine bark habitat for lichens can be a harsh environment. The bark is very acidic, tends to be quite dry and flakes off easily and often. The presence of this and other lichens on the bark may actually provide a means of cementing protective bark to the tree.

trees

crustose

Brown-eyed Rim Lichen   *Lecanora allophana*

trees

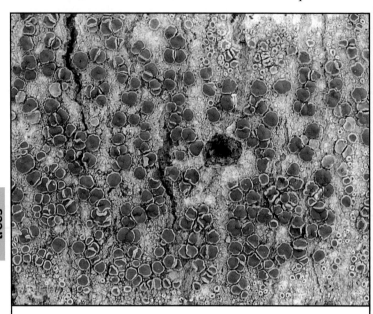

Grows on bark, especially poplar and ash.

crustose

Nature Notes:

Lecanora has many look-alikes. This is a great example of the value of using chemistry and microscopes for identification purposes. More than half of all lichen species world-wide are crustose. Distinct apothecial disks make this genus, *Lecanora*, recognizable. Identifying *Lecanora* to species is another task altogether. Many of the 171 species of *Lecanora* in North America look alike and are only divided by using complex micro-chemical tests.

Description: Crustose grayish surface with reddish brown disks.

Thallus: Grayish.

Apothecia: Large reddish-brown disks 2mm diameter.

Chemistry: Thallus K+ yellow (atranorin and triterpenes).

Similar Species: There are 171 species of *Lecanora* in North America. Let's face it they all look alike.

Mapledust Lichen   *Lecanora thysanophora*

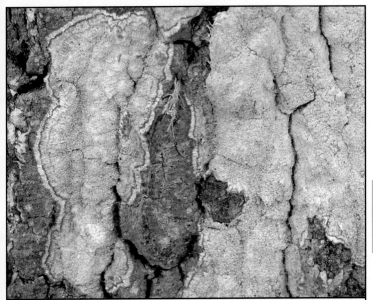

Grows on Sugar Maple, but also on beech, oak and basswood.

Description: Crustose pale green to yellowish-green surface with a white to bluish webby margin.

Thallus: Pale green to yellowish green with a white webby margin.

Apothecia: Rarely seen.

Chemistry: Thallus K+ yellow and KC+ gold (usnic acid, atranorin and zeorin).

Similar Species: Although it does look a bit like a yellowish-green Dust Lichen (*Lepraria*), look for the white webby margins of Mapledust to confirm your identification.

Nature Notes:

Look at the white edges —the fungal partner. The green granular surface is a result of the algal partner. Younger maples with smooth bark are ideal sites. As maple bark ages it begins to ooze alkaline, nitrogenous compounds, which alter the lichen community resulting in a more diverse community.

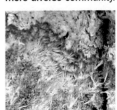

trees

crustose

Bark Disk Lichen *Lecidela euphorea*

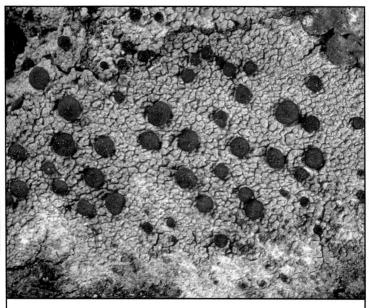

Grows on bark.

trees

crustose

Nature Notes:

Crustose lichens are by far the dominant group of lichens. They are commonly referred to as the microlichens because of the need to use a microscope for accurate identification. Approximately 55 percent of all lichens worldwide are crustose with the remaining 45 percent divided between foliose and fruticose species.

Description: Crustose thin gray-green or white surface with black disks.

Thallus: Gray-green or white and thin.

Apothecia: Black disks 0.4-1.2mm diameter.

Chemistry: Thallus K+ pale orange (zeorin and atranorin).

Similar Species: It can be difficult to separate this lichen from other black disk lichens such as *Lecidea* and *Porpidia*.

Fluffy Dust Lichen   *Lepraria lobificans*

Common on tree bases and shaded rock.

trees

Description: Crustose yellowish-green to pale mint granular, fuzzy or dusty surface.

Thallus: Yellowish-green to pale mint green, thick and cottony.

Apothecia: None.

Chemistry: Thallus PD+ orange and K+ yellow (atronorin, zeorin, stictic and constictic acids).

Similar Species: Mapledust (*Lecanora thysanophora*) has a distinct white, webby margin.

Nature Notes:

Lichen names are revisited on occasion and changed to reflect the current worldview on any particular species' definition. This species was once called *Lepraria finkii* in honor of Bruce Fink, a highly regarded lichenologist of the early 1900s. Fink was a leader in lichenology in North America. He wrote *Lichens of Minnesota* in 1910 and then *Lichen Flora of the United States* in 1935. Many of the earliest records of lichens collected in northern MN are those collected by Bruce Fink.

crustose

Bloody Heart Lichen   *Mycoblastus sanguinarius*

Grows on bark and wood of conifer and birch.

trees

crustose

Nature Notes:

Use a razor blade to slice through the surface of the black apothecia and you'll find a bright red zone of pigment...or you won't. If the "bloody heart" is present (photo below), you can't confuse this with any other lichen.

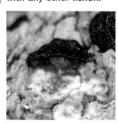

Description: Crustose grayish-white to greenish gray surface with shiny black hemispherical disks.

Thallus: White, thick surface.

Apothecia: Black disks 2.5mm diameter with a bright red zone just below the surface (slice through this with a razor blade).

Chemistry: Thallus K+ yellow (atranorin and caperatic acid).

Similar Species: White Heart Lichen (*Mycoblastus affinis*) lacks red pigment in its apothecia.

Rosy Saucer Lichen *Ochrolechia trochophora*

Grows on bark of deciduous trees and Northern White Cedar.

Description: Crustose gray surface with rosy to yellowish-pink disks.

Thallus: Gray.

Apothecia: Rosy to yellowish-pink disks 0.8-3mm diameter.

Chemistry: Thallus C+ pink (gyrophoric acid).

Similar Species: *Lecanora* and *Pertusaria* will occasionally resemble this lichen.

Nature Notes:

Also known as "cudbear," this genus of lichen contains gyrophoric acid which yields a purple dye under fermentation. From 1758 to 1810, the Cuthbert family in Scotland scraped *Ochrolechia* lichens from rock (a different species than this one) until the resource was gone. Yet another example of overextending our resources. Rock Tripe (*Umbilicaria*) replaced it as a source of purple dye.

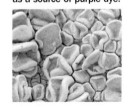

trees

crustose

Bitter Wart Lichen *Pertusaria amara*

Grows on bark of both hardwoods and conifers.

trees

crustose

Nature Notes:

The bitter taste of Bitter Wart Lichen was the basis for its use in controlling high fever. Presumably, the bitter quality was like quinine and assumed to be similar in other respects. A tiny bit, when chewed will produce a very bitter taste that lasts for a long time. Fortunately, it's not poisonous and bitterness can be safely used for identification.

Description: Crustose gray to greenish-gray coarse surface.

Thallus: Gray to greenish-gray coarse and granular surface.

Apothecia: Buried in thallus warts.

Chemistry: Thallus KC+ purple (picrolichenic acid).

Similar Species: Ragged Wart Lichen (*Pertusaria ophthalmiza*) has a thin and smooth, pale gray surface with broad fruiting disks and no lichen chemistry. There are 75 species of *Pertusaria* in North America.

Whitewash Lichen *Phlyctis argena*

Grows on bark of deciduous trees (especially Northern White Cedar and Red Maple) and occasionally conifers.

Description: Crustose smooth white surface.

Thallus: Smooth white surface.

Apothecia: Extremely uncommon.

Chemistry: Thallus PD+ yellow and K+ yellow changing to blood-red (norstictic acid).

Similar Species: Whitewash Lichen looks like many white crustose lichens. Look for evidence of reproductive structures with any semblance of color in order to eliminate this species.

Nature Notes:

It looks as though Tom Sawyer ran through the forest with his band of whitewashing hoodlums randomly applying their paintbrushes to tree trunks. This is very common in our region, especially on cedar and red maple. Without apothecia and looking sterile, it is remarkable that it can reproduce at all. In fact, it reproduces with soredia, which are tiny granules of the algal component wrapped in a gauze of fungal tissues. When soredia are brushed away to another suitable substrate, they have all that is needed to produce another white swath of paint on the bark.

trees

crustose

Eastern Candlewax Lichen *Ahtiana aurescens*

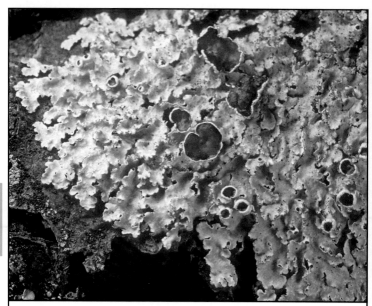

Grows on cedars and pines, rarely hardwoods.

trees

foliose

Nature Notes:

Recorded in only 17 localities in Michigan, Minnesota and Wisconsin since 1970, the main threats to this species include logging, blowdowns and roads that damage old-growth forests. Old-growth forests provide a unique composite of shade, substrate texture and localized humidity. Lichens serve foresters and ecologists as a natural tool with which to monitor forest conditions and health.

When found, this species is often growing alongside American Starburst Lichen (*Imshaugia placorodia*) on pines.

Description: Foliose yellowish-green overlapping lobes growing closely to the substrate with a pale brown, shiny lower surface.

Thallus: Yellowish-green overlapping lobes 0.5-2mm wide with a shiny, pale brown lower surface.

Apothecia: Abundant, red-brown disks 2-7mm diameter somewhat raised from the surface.

Chemistry: Cortex KC+ yellow (usnic acid).

Similar Species: Yellow Ribbon Lichen (*Allocetraria oakesiana*) is similar in many respects except for the yellowish soredia on the margins.

Candleflame Lichen *Candelaria concolor*

Grows along rain tracks on tree trunks.

trees

Description: Foliose, small bright yellow rosettes with overlapping lobes.

Thallus: Bright yellow rosettes (<1cm diameter) with overlapping irregularly arranged lobes 0.1-0.5mm wide.

Apothecia: Uncommon dark yellow to orange-brown disks 0.2-0.7mm diameter.

Chemistry: Apothecia K+ pink (calycin).

Similar Species: Fringed Candleflame Lichen (*Candelaria fibrosa*) has a yolk-yellow thallus with radiating lobes 0.3-0.5mm wide and apothecia are very common, to 2mm diameter and darker yellow.

Nature Notes:

Calycin is a pulvinic acid derivative—like the vulpinic acid found in *Vulpicida* and *Cyphelium*. These lichen substances are responsible for the yellow pigment. They also serve as a sunscreen to protect the delicate algae, *Trebouxia*, that grows more robust at low light levels. This adaptive advantage helps to make this species one of the most common tree lichens throughout the entire Temperate Element (see Lichen Biology 101).

This species is sensitive to sulphur dioxide.

foliose

Tree Jelly Lichen   *Collema subflaccidum*

Grows on bark of hardwoods, especially in old forests, also growing on shaded mossy rocks.

trees

foliose

Nature Notes:

The dark color of this lichen indicates the presence of cyanobacteria and the ability to capture and utilize atmospheric nitrogen. Access to nitrogen limits the growth of many organisms. Carnivorous plants, such as sundew and pitcher plant, extract nitrogen from their prey. Alders, Sphagnum Moss and legumes form symbiotic relationships with a variety of nitrogen-fixing bacteria. Symbiosis is everywhere!

Description: Foliose dark olive to almost black rounded lobes.

Thallus: Dark olive to almost black lobes 2-6mm wide with rounded ends.

Apothecia: Rarely seen.

Chemistry: No lichen substances.

Similar Species: Jelly Flakes (*Collema undulatum*) has divided lobes and is limited to rock surfaces.

Common Greenshield *Flavoparmelia caperata*

Grows on bark of all kinds in sun or partial shade.

trees

Description: Foliose pale yellow-green lobes with black lower surface and pale brown under edges.

Thallus: Pale yellow-green lobes 3-8mm wide.

Apothecia: Rare.

Chemistry: Medulla PD+ red-orange and KC+ gold (atranorin and usnic, protocetraric and caperatic acids).

Similar Species: Speckled Greenshield (*Flavopunctelia flavientor*) has white pores on the upper surface and the medulla is C+ red (lecanoric acid). Rock Greenshield (*Flavoparmelia baltimorensis*) has pustule-like outgrowths on the upper surface and grows exclusively on rocks.

Nature Notes:

These lichens are extremely common. As a rule, lichens have a low diversity and abundance in urban and industrial areas due to atmospheric pollution. After a complete loss of lichens in polluted areas, some of the first noticeable lichens to return are those of the Greenshield group.

In favorable habitats Greenshield may grow as much as 5mm per year (See illustration on page 14).

foliose

Hooded Tube Lichen *Hypogymnia physodes*

Grows on bark and wood of conifers.

Nature Notes:

Lichens are valued as biomonitoring agents of air quality in three ways:
1) Mapping all species in an area and following the changes over time.
2) Transplanting healthy lichens into a polluted area and monitoring their development.
3) Sampling an individual species over a wide area then measuring pollutants in their thallus.

Description: Foliose pale greenish-gray smooth lobes fanning at the tips.

Thallus: Pale greenish gray smooth lobes fanning at tips 1-5mm wide. Lower surface is black without rhizines.

Apothecia: Rare.

Chemistry: Medulla PD+ red (physodalic, protocetraric and physodic acids).

Similar Species: Powder-headed Tube Lichen (*Hypogymnia tubulosa*) is a greenish-gray lichen usually under 4cm diameter with lobes 0.5-3mm wide. The tips of lobes remain closed. Growing on conifer twigs, also on birch or alder bark.

trees

foliose

American Starburst Lichen *Imshaugia placorodia*

Grows on Jack Pine.

Description: Foliose pale gray lobes with a creamy white to pale brown lower surface and pale brown disks abundant in the center.

Thallus: Pale gray lobes 0.5-1.5mm wide and lower surface creamy white to pale brown with short, brown rhizines.

Apothecia: Pale brown concave disks 2-7mm diameter abundant in the center.

Chemistry: Thallus PD+ orange and K+ deep yellow (thamnolic acid).

Similar Species: There are two species worldwide. Salted Starburst Lichen (*Imshaugia aleurites*) grows in circular patches of white to pale gray, shiny lobes. Apothecia are rare. This species is found growing on conifer bark in well-lit forests.

Nature Notes:

Both species of Starburst Lichens are restricted to pine bark. This harsh environment is very acidic, tends to be very dry and flakes off easily and often.

The genus is named in honor of Henry Imshaug, of Michigan State University. He collected specimens of fungi, mosses, liverworts and lichens broadly over the world from 1958 to 1990.

trees

foliose

Lungwort *Lobaria pulmonaria*

Grows on trees, mossy rocks and wood in mature woodlands. Found in rich, unpolluted and often very old forests.

trees

foliose

Nature Notes:

Herbals list this lichen as a good remedy for tuberculosis—perhaps because of its resemblance to lung tissue.

A monastery in Siberia had a reputation for serving bitter and highly intoxicating beer to travelers. The recipe replaced hops with lungwort.

Lobaria has been used in the tanning of animal hides due to the astringent property of its depsides.

Lungwort is a favorite food of moose in the northeast.

It is sensitive to sulphur dioxide levels in the atmosphere above 10 parts per billion.

Description: Foliose pale brown to olive-brown large lobes with distinct ridges and pits on the surface.

Thallus: Pale brown to olive-brown when dry (turning strongly green when wet—see above), lobes 8-30mm wide and up to 7cm long. The upper surface is strongly ridged and pitted.

Apothecia: Infrequently found near the lobe margins.

Chemistry: Medulla PD+ orange or yellow and K+ red (stictic and norstictic acids).

Similar Species: Although it is related to Smooth Lungwort (*Lobaria quercizans*), the two look nothing alike.

dry

Smooth Lungwort   *Lobaria quercizans*

Grows on bark of Sugar Maple, sometimes on mossy rock.

trees

Description: Foliose gray, smooth squarish lobes with distinct red-brown disks scattered on the surface.

Thallus: Gray, smooth lobes 6-20mm wide.

Apothecia: Numerous red-brown disks up to 4.5mm diameter scattered on thallus surface.

Chemistry: Cortex K+ yellow with medulla K+ orange and C+ pink (atranorin and gyrophoric acid).

Similar Species: The large lobes and numerous red-brown apothecia set this lichen apart from all others in the North Woods.

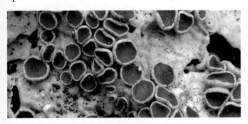

Nature Notes:

Smooth Lungwort is one of the 11 species of concern in the North Woods. The main threat to its survival is large-scale logging that would eliminate large tracts of old-growth Sugar Maple, Yellow Birch and Black Ash. It is commonly found on trees exceeding 100 years old. Trees older than 150 years may have thalli 50-60 years old. This species is important in the fixation of nitrogen. Look for evidence of the internal cephalodia that can be seen as small bumps on the lower surface.

foliose

Abraded Camouflage Lichen *Melanelia subaurifera*

Grows on bark of all kinds, rarely rock.

Nature Notes:

The dark surface provides protection from intense light from the sun for the green algae, *Trebouxia*. It may also absorb the sunlight's warmth during winter to provide optimum temperatures for respiration and growth.

Description: Foliose olive to chocolate brown dull many-branched lobes.

Thallus: Olive to chocolate brown, dull lobes 1-4mm wide.

Apothecia: Uncommon.

Chemistry: Medulla C+ red (lecanoric acid).

Similar Species: Other Camouflage Lichens (*Melanelia*) likely have apothecia.

Spotted Camouflage Lichen   *Melanelia olivacea*

Grows on birch.

Description: Foliose dark olive to olive-brown heavily wrinkled lobes with abundant, elevated and somewhat concave disks of the same color.

Thallus: Dark olive to olive-brown heavily wrinkled surface with lobes 2-5mm wide and a black lower surface with many rhizines.

Apothecia: A few disks 1.5-5mm diameter elevated and somewhat concave.

Chemistry: Medulla PD+ red (fumarprotocetraric acid).

Similar Species: Northern Camouflage Lichen (*Melanelia septentrionalis*) has a brown thallus closely attached to bark of all trees. Apothecia are broad, flattened and shiny yellowish.

Nature Notes:

Only found on birch. Birchbark provides a substrate very similar to pine bark—acidic and flaky. As such, you can expect to see a community of lichens on birch that would be very similar to that on spruce, pine and fir.

A very common species of the boreal forest and widely distributed throughout the northern hemisphere including Scandinavia and Siberia.

trees

foliose

Treeflute Lichen   *Menagazzia terrebrata*

Grows on bark of deciduous trees and cedar in damp forests.

Nature Notes:

Other names include Magic Treeflute and Porthole Lichen.

Listed as threatened in the Great Lakes region and Red-listed in Europe. The greatest threats to survival are air pollution, logging, road construction, overgrowth by mosses and excessive shade. Only 20 reports of it in Minnesota, 2 in Wisconsin and 10 in Michigan.

Since it grows in cedar swamps, one would think it would be safe. However, due to deer browse and lack of cedar regeneration, this species may be at greater risk than thought.

Description: Foliose light mineral gray, smooth puffy lobes with large round pores in the upper surface into the hollow interior.

Thallus: Light mineral gray smooth puffy lobes 1-2mm wide with large round pores open into the hollow interior. Lower surface black, wrinkled and without rhizines.

Apothecia: Rare.

Chemistry: Cortex K+ yellow with medulla PD+ orange and K+ dark yellow (atranorin and stictic, menagazziaic and constictic acids).

Similar Species: Small individuals with few perforations may be mistaken with the Tube Lichens (*Hypogymnia*).

trees

foliose

Smooth Axil-bristle Lichen *Myelochroa galbina*

Grows on bark of deciduous trees and rarely rock.

Description: Foliose pale gray to blue-gray lobes with reddish-brown disks.

Thallus: Blue-gray lobes 0.8-2mm wide with black lower surface and abundant black rhizines.

Apothecia: Reddish-brown disks.

Chemistry: Medulla PD+ orange and K+ yellow to red (galbanic acid).

Similar Species: Rock Axil-bristle Lichen (*Myelochroa obsessa*) is restricted to rocks. Powdery Axil-bristle Lichen (*Myelochroa aurulenta*) grows on trees, but has soredia on the upper surface.

Nature Notes:

Rhizines can vary greatly among all the lichens. They are a fungal growth that generally serves to attach the foliose lichens to their substrate. They can have varying manners of branching, length, thickness and color. Pull out your hand lens, or better yet put a sample of this lichen under a microscope for a closer inspection.

"Axil-bristle" refers to the rhizines.

trees

foliose

Bottlebrush Shield Lichen   *Parmelia squarrosa*

Grows on bark or mossy rock in mostly shade and sun.

trees

foliose

Nature Notes:

The Shield Lichens are perhaps the most common and obvious lichens in the North Woods. They are the first organisms to colonize trees and even picnic tables.

Some *Parmelia* are know by dyers as crottle, a source of deep red-brown dyes.

Ruby-throated Hummingbirds camouflage the outer surface of their nests with bits of *Parmelia*.

Description: Foliose pale gray surface with overlapping lobes.

Thallus: Pale gray upper surface with overlapping lobes 1-5mm wide. Lower surface black with branched rhizines.

Apothecia: Can be common.

Chemistry: Medulla PD+ yellow and K+ yellow turning blood-red (salazinic and consalazinic acids).

Similar Species: Hammered Shield Lichen (*Parmelia sulcata*) has blue-gray lobes 2-5mm wide with a network of sharp ridges and depressions. The lower surface is black with unbranched rhizines and apothecia are rare.

Green Starburst Lichen *Parmeliopsis ambigua*

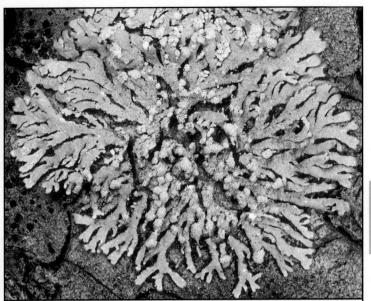

Grows on conifer stumps, logs and bark in full sun.

Description: Foliose pale yellowish-green radiating lobes with a brown to almost black lower surface.

Thallus: Pale yellowish-green radiating lobes 0.5-2mm wide. Lower surface brown to almost black with rhizines.

Apothecia: Uncommon.

Chemistry: Medulla UV+ blue-white (divaricatic and usnic acids).

Similar Species: Gray Starburst Lichen (*Parmeliopsis hyperopta*) has a pale gray thallus with cortex PD+ light yellow and K+ yellow (atranorin and divaricatic acid).

Nature Notes:

Green Starburst Lichen and Gray Starburst Lichen grow side-by-side on weathered old wood, especially conifer wood and bark.

There are only three species of *Parmeliopsis* in North America.

trees

foliose

Orange-cored Shadow Lichen *Phaeophyscia rubropulchr*

Grows on bark of deciduous trees in shaded forests and rarely conifers, moss or rock.

trees

foliose

Nature Notes:

Foliose lichens have several layers: the upper cortex, a photobiont layer, a medulla and a lower cortex with rhizines. This is one of the best examples for seeing the medulla, or internal layer composed of loosely packed fungal tissue. Carefully scrape away the upper cortex with a knife or fingernail to reveal the red-orange inner core. This is a typical lichen of the Eastern Temperate Element.

Description: Foliose pale to dark green or dark brown small-lobed surface with red-orange inner core.

Thallus: Pale to dark green or dark brown lobes 0.5-1.2mm wide with slightly upturned tips. Lower surface black and rhizines have white tips. Medulla red-brown.

Apothecia: Common dark brown to almost black disks under 1mm diameter.

Chemistry: Medulla K+ purple (anthraquinone).

Similar Species: Many Rosette Lichens (*Physcia*) can be confused with Shadow Lichens, however they tend to have a grayer surface and test K+ yellow on the upper surface.

Powder-tipped Shadow Lichen *Phaeophyscia adiastola*

Grows on bark and mossy granitic rock.

trees

Description: Foliose dark greenish-gray to brown lobes with a black lower surface.

Thallus: Dark greenish-gray to brown lobes 0.5-1mm wide. Lower surface black with abundant white tipped rhizines.

Apothecia: Rare.

Chemistry: No lichen substances.

Similar Species: Many Rosette Lichens (*Physcia*) can be confused with Shadow Lichens, however they tend to have a grayer surface and test K+ yellow on the upper surface.

Nature Notes:

Trebouxia is the most common green algae found in lichen symbioses. The genus is represented by unicellular, usually spherical alga containing a large stellate (star-like) chloroplast. Although it is most widespread as the photobiont in lichens of all sorts, they are not obligated to this growth and can be found in nature on tree bark.

foliose

Pom-pom Shadow Lichen *Phaeophyscia pusillodes*

trees

Grows on bark of all kinds.

foliose

Nature Notes:

Rhizines can vary greatly among all the lichens. They are a fungal growth that generally serves to attach the foliose lichens to their substrate. They can have varying manners of branching, length, thickness and color. Pull out your hand lens, or better yet put a sample of any of the Shadow Lichens under a microscope for a closer inspection.

Description: Foliose greenish-gray to brown overlapping lobes with rhizines often extending out beyond the edges of the thallus.

Thallus: Greenish-gray to brown with overlapping lobes less than 1mm wide. The black lower surface has black rhizines often extending out on all sides

Apothecia: Uncommon.

Chemistry: No lichen substances.

Similar Species: Many Rosette Lichens (*Physcia*) can be confused with Shadow Lichens, however they tend to have a grayer surface and test K+ yellow on the upper surface.

Hooded Rosette Lichen   *Physcia adscendens*

Grows on bark and twigs, less frequently on rock.

Description: Foliose pale gray to greenish lichen with white spots. The narrow lobes have inflated hoods and long white hairs at the tips.

Thallus: Pale gray to greenish-gray surface with white spots and a white lower surface. Lobes 1mm wide with inflated hoods at tips and long, white cilia.

Apothecia: Not common.

Chemistry: Thallus K+ yellow (atranorin and triterpenes).

Similar Species: Some specimens of *Phaeophyscia*, *Physconia*, *Parmeliopsis* and *Imshaugia* can be confusing. Most small, light gray foliose lichens with a pale lower surface and K+ yellow thallus are Rosette Lichens (*Physcia*).

Nature Notes:

A climate is defined by the average weather over a long period. Small variations in the larger landscape can be a result of terrain or aspect such as a north facing cliff. Smaller yet, this lichen shows a strong relationship to the microclimates on a tree trunk—extremely small changes in humidity, available sunlight and wind. Hooded Rosette Lichen decreases in abundance as you move higher up the trunk. In contrast, Hoary Rosette Lichen (*Physcia aipolia*) increases in abundance as you move up the tree trunk.

trees

foliose

Star Rosette Lichen   *Physcia stellaris*

Grows on poplar, elm and alder bark.

trees

Nature Notes:

During the 15th century, there was a strong following of a medical belief—the Doctrine of Signatures—which stated simply that plants having resemblance to parts of the human body or to a particular disease must in turn produce a cure. One species of *Physcia* (at the time called *Mucus cranii humani*) was found growing on human skulls. "Skull" lichen was worth its weight in gold as a cure for epilepsy.

foliose

Description: Foliose pale gray rosette with a darker center and dark brown disks.

Thallus: Pale gray rosette with a darker center and radiating lobes 0.5-1.5mm wide. The lower white surface has fairly abundant rhizines.

Apothecia: Common dark brown disks 0.7-3mm diameter.

Chemistry: Cortex and thallus K+ yellow (atranorin).

Similar Species: Some specimens of *Phaeophyscia*, *Physconia*, *Parmeliopsis* and *Imshaugia* can be confusing. Most small, light gray foliose lichens with a pale lower surface and K+ yellow thallus are Rosette Lichens (*Physcia*).

N. Bottlebrush Frost Lichen *Physconia leucolyptes*

trees

Grows on bark of various kinds of trees, rarely on rock.

Description: Foliose pale gray-brown to dark red-brown lobes with shiny upper surface and a black lower surface with a thick mat of rhizines.

Thallus: Pale gray-brown to dark red-brown with shiny lobes 1.2mm wide slightly upturned at tips. Black lower surface with thick mat of black rhizines.

Apothecia: Rare.

Chemistry: Medulla K+ yellow and soredia K+ yellow (secalonic acid).

Similar Species: Bottlebrush Frost Lichen (*Physconia detersa*) has no positive lichen chemistry tests.

Nature Notes:

Lichen chemistry plays a large role in both the lichen's survival and identification. Secalonic acids are extremely toxic and most likely serve as a deterrent to potential herbivores.

The presence and resulting K+ yellow reaction helps to separate the two species of Bottlebrush Frost Lichens.

foliose

Crumpled Rag Lichen *Platismatia tuckermanii*

Grows on bark and wood of conifers.

Nature Notes:

Tuckermanii is in reference to Edward Tuckerman, the pre-eminent lichenologist of the mid-1800s.

This lichen, like the Wrinkle Lichens (*Tuckermanopsis*), is adapted to take advantage of rainwater running down the branches of its conifer host. This provides moisture and also transports some nutrients leeched from the bark higher above.

Description: Foliose pale gray to greenish-gray crumpled lobes with shiny red-brown disks on lobe margins.

Thallus: Pale gray to greenish-gray lobes 4-20mm wide with brown to black edges and a crumpled appearance. The lower surface is usually uniformly shiny brown.

Apothecia: Common shiny red-brown 2-10mm diameter disks on lobe margins.

Chemistry: Cortex K+ yellow (caperatic acid and atranorin).

Similar Species: Fringed Wrinkle Lichen (*Tuckermanopsis americana*) has a very similar growth pattern—crumpled looking lobes rising from twigs. *Tuckermanopsis* is distinctly brownish and the lobes grow no larger than 6mm wide.

trees

foliose

Yellow Specklebelly *Pseudocyphellaria crocata*

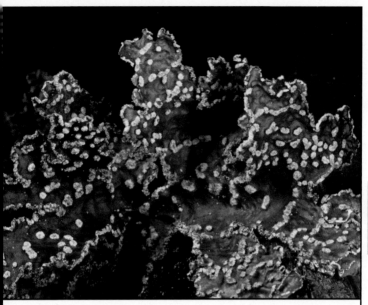

Grows on bark, shrubs and mossy rock in humid sites.

Description: Foliose greenish-gray to dark brown lichen with white or yellow dots on the surface.

Thallus: Pale to dark chocolate brown lobes 5-20mm wide with bright yellow spots on lower ridge.

Apothecia: Rare.

Chemistry: PD+ orange, K+ yellow.

Similar Species: Peppered Moon Lichen (*Sticta fuliginosa*), another very rare lichen in our area on the list of special concern, has white spots among the abundant tomentum. It also favors old growth yellow birch.

Nature Notes:

One of 11 lichen species in 2007 listed as special concern in the Lakes State's National Forests, there have only been four records of this species since 1979: on a large boulder in Voyageurs National Park, on Devil's Island in Lake Superior, on a leaning Yellow Birch on Isle Royale and the most recent on a Northern White Cedar in Patterson Hemlocks Scientific & Natural Area in northern Wisconsin.

Yellow Specklebelly is named for the yellow "speckles" (dots) on the "belly" (upper lobes surfaces).

trees

foliose

Rough Speckled Shield Lichen   *Punctelia rudecta*

Grows on bark of all kinds or on shaded rock.

Nature Notes:

Isidia are structures that provide for vegetative reproduction. They are essentially finger-like projections from the lichen thallus that contain a bit of the algae wrapped up in fungal tissue. Isidia can be brushed off, leaving a scar, and then regenerate into a new lichen thallus.

Speckled Shield Lichens are most common to cedar bark and many deciduous trees.

Description: Foliose dark greenish-gray to almost blue-gray speckled lobes with a pale tan lower surface.

Thallus: Dark greenish-gray to almost blue-gray lobes 3-8mm wide with white isidia. Pale tan lower surface with pale rhizines.

Apothecia: Uncommon.

Chemistry: Medulla C+ red (lecanoric acid).

Similar Species: Powdered Speckled Shield Lichen (*Punctelia subrudecta*) is dark greenish gray often browned at the edges.

Peppered Moon Lichen *Sticta fuliginosa*

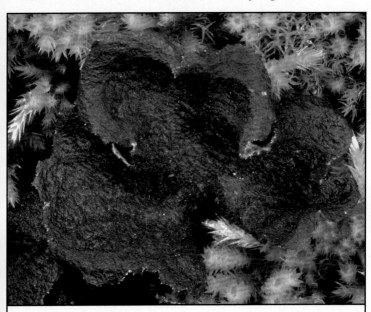

Grows on mossy bark.

Description: Foliose dark brown to olive-gray lobes with a crinkled upper surface and a pale brown fuzzy lower surface.

Thallus: Dark brown to olive-gray with lobes 7-15mm wide. Upper surface crinkled and lower surface pale brown and fuzzy with distinct white pits. The entire thallus can grow to 5-10cm across.

Apothecia: Rare.

Chemistry: No lichen substances.

Similar Species: Yellow Specklebelly (*Pseudocyphellaria crocata*) is another rare lichen in the North Woods. It has distinct bright yellow spots on the lower ridges.

Nature Notes:

This Moon Lichen favors old Yellow Birch in very humid old growth areas. It is very sensitive to air pollution and can fix nitrogen.

The loss of *Sticta fuliginosa* in our area is due mainly to logging of old-growth forests and to a lesser degree from air pollution, especially sulphur dioxide levels higher than 11 parts per billion.

trees

foliose

Fringed Wrinkle Lichen *Tuckermanopsis americana*

Grows on twigs and branches of conifers and birch in exposed sites.

Nature Notes:

Named for Edward Tuckerman (1817-1886), the pre-eminent founder and promoter of lichenology in North America. As a botanist and professor in Boston, he did most of his plant studies on Mount Washington and in the White Mountains. He published *North American Lichens* (1881, 1888). There was a movement to create a lichen society called "Tuckermania."

wet

Description: Foliose dark brown to olive-brown ascending wrinkled lobes with similarly colored disks.

Thallus: Dark brown to olive-brown when dry, greenish when wet, ascending lobes 3-6mm wide. The lower surface pale to dark brown and wrinkled.

Apothecia: Common 7mm diameter disks resembling thallus.

Chemistry: Cortex K+ yellow (atranorin) and medulla UV+ blue-white (alectoronic acid).

Similar Species: Chestnut Wrinkle Lichen (*Tuckermanopsis sepincola*) is a yellow-brown to red-brown lichen forming rounded cushions under 2cm diameter growing near water. This lichen has no positive lichen chemistry.

Powdered Sunshine Lichen   *Vulpicida pinastri*

Grows on bark, wood and rock in open and shaded sites.

Description: Foliose greenish-yellow to bright yellow lobes with ruffled edges.

Thallus: Greenish-yellow to bright yellow rosette with ruffled lobes 1.5-5mm wide. The lower surface is pale yellow to almost white.

Apothecia: Uncommon.

Chemistry: No reliable tests. Contains usnic, vulpinic and pinastric acids as well as zeorin.

Similar Species: Yellow Ribbon Lichen (*Allocetraria oakesiana*) is more greenish and very rare.

Nature Notes:

Vulpes is the Latin name for fox. *Cide* refers to death.

Wolf Lichen (*Letharia vulpina*) has been used in Northern Europe to kill wolves and foxes. The toxin, vulpinic acid, is poisonous to a variety of animals. The concentrated toxin was mixed with crushed glass and placed into the bait.

Powdered Sunshine Lichen seems to grow no higher than chest height. Perhaps protective snowdrifts shield the lichen from dry winter winds.

trees

foliose

Poplar Sunburst Lichen *Xanthoria hasseana*

Grows on bark, especially aspen, in open or partially shaded sites.

Nature Notes:

Parietin is a substance likely offering a form of sunscreen, especially from UV-B radiation. This pigment is often darker in the direct sun and faded in the shadows.

Description: Foliose yellow-orange to orange rosette with a white lower surface and bright orange disks confined to the center.

Thallus: Yellow-orange to orange loosely attached rosettes with lobes 0.3-0.9mm wide. The white lower surface has abundant rhizines.

Apothecia: Bright orange disks 0.6-3mm diameter confined to center of thallus.

Chemistry: Medulla K+ deep red-purple (parietin).

Similar Species: Pin-cushion Sunburst Lichen (*Xanthoria polycarpa*) forms small yellow-orange to orange cushions (2.5cm diameter) with abundant thallus-colored apothecia crowding the center. It is most often found growing on bark, especially twigs and branches of spruce, oak and fir.

Powdery Sunburst Lichen *Xanthoria ulophyllodes*

Grows on oak, maple and elm, rarely on rock.

Description: Foliose yellow-orange to orange radiating lobes with white lower surface.

Thallus: Yellow-orange to orange radiating, branched lobes 0.3-1.4mm wide. Upper surface is powdery on margins and sometimes over large areas with a white lower surface and abundant rhizines.

Apothecia: Uncommon.

Chemistry: K+ deep red-purple (parietin).

Similar Species: Hooded Sunburst Lichen (*Xanthoria fallax*) has short, rounded lobes 0.8-2mm wide and lacks the powdery surface.

Nature Notes:

As with many organisms, nitrogen is a limiting factor in the growth and abundance of the *Xanthoria* species. The Sunburst Lichens growing on trees get all their needs from the air. Next to farmland where fertilizers are applied, these orange lichens are more prevalent. Nitrogenous compounds may also drip from tree bark or lichens above during a rain.

trees

foliose

Moosehair Lichen   *Bryoria trichodes*

Grows on conifers and birches in forests, open bogs and along lakeshores.

Nature Notes:

Moosehair Lichen is also known as Horsehair Lichen or Pine Moss.

Horsehair (*Bryoria*), Bushy (*Ramalina*) and Beard (*Usnea*) Lichens are among those arboreal lichens particularly sensitive to air pollution. A forest heavily covered in these lichens is very likely indicative of high air quality.

Deer, moose, squirrels and red-backed voles all eat *Bryoria* lichens.

Aboriginal peoples of the Far North made a gelatinous black paste shaped into biscuits for food.

Description: Fruticose dark brown to pale gray-brown draping hair-like branches.

Thallus: Pale to dark brown draping smooth branches 7-15cm long and 0.1-0.4mm diameter.

Apothecia: Frequently along branches with pale reddish-brown disks.

Chemistry: Inner cortex PD+ red (fumarprotocetraric acid).

Similar Species: Burred Horsehair Lichen (*Bryoria furcelata*) is a shiny dark brown lichen forming bushy clumps up to 5cm across with short side branches. *Bryoria furcelata* rarely has apothecia.

trees

fruticose

Boreal Oakmoss   *Evernia mesomorpha*

trees

Grows on branches and trunks of all trees in sunny sites.

Description: Fruticose pale yellowish-green abundantly branched and loosely hanging stalks.

Thallus: Forming hanging to shrubby tufts 4-8cm long with wrinkled branches 0.5-1.5mm diameter.

Apothecia: Rare.

Chemistry: No positive tests. Contains divaricatic acid and usnic acid.

Similar Species: Beard Lichens (*Usnea*) tend to be thinner with several side branches and Bushy Lichens (*Ramalina*) are flattened.

Nature Notes:

Oakmoss (*Evernia*) is more pollution-tolerant than Beard Lichen (*Usnea*). Consequently, you will find it closer to urban areas.

Usnic acid is a common substance found in many lichens. For some, contact with skin can result in a severe rash known as "woodcutter's eczema" or "cedar poisoning."

fruticose

Common Antler Lichen   *Pseudevernia consocians*

Grows on conifers in forests.

Nature Notes:

Pseudevernia furfuracea and *P. prunastri* are common European species that are sources of fragrances and fixatives in the perfume and cosmetic industry in France. Nearly 10,000 tons of this lichen are harvested annually in France, Morocco and former Yugoslavia. Imagine the devastation to our forest systems if this were an industry in North America.

Description: Fruticose pale gray flattened branches.

Thallus: Pale gray with flattened lobes 1-1.5mm wide. The lobe surface is abundantly covered with isidia.

Apothecia: Rare.

Chemistry: Medulla C+ pink to red (lecanoric acid).

Similar Species: Boreal Oakmoss (*Evernia mesomorpha*) is obviously green in contrast to the pale gray of the Common Antler Lichen.

trees

fruticose

Sinewed Bushy Lichen *Ramalina americana*

Grows on twigs and branches of various trees in full sun.

Description: Fruticose yellowish-green shrubby to draping branches.

Thallus: Yellowish-green in tufts 1-3cm long, branches .5-3mm wide with strong ridges. The thallus is solid in cross section.

Apothecia: Yellow disks at or near branch tips.

Chemistry: Cortex KC+ dark yellow (usnic acid).

Similar Species: Punctured Bushy Lichen (*Ramalina dilacerata*) grows on twigs and branches of all sorts of trees, typically on lakeshores, but the hollow thallus is rather smooth with many perforations into the medulla. Rock Bushy Lichen (*Ramalina intermedia*) will grow only on rock.

Nature Notes:

Ramalina, Usnea and *Bryoria* are among those arboreal lichens particularly sensitive to air pollutants.

The most common pigment in lichens—usnic acid—produces the light yellow in this lichen. Usnic acid serves to protect lichens against shortwave UV light. The UV light can damage sensitive algae.

trees

fruticose

Bristly Beard Lichen   *Usnea hirta*

Very common on coniferous trees and birch.

Nature Notes:

According to the Doctrine of Signatures, Beard Lichens (*Usnea*) could be used to treat diseases of the scalp.

Usnic acid does have antibiotic properties and has been reported in some studies to be more effective than penicillin in the treatment of external wounds and burns.

Description: Fruticose pale yellowish-green densely branched small, shrubby main stems with dense short side branches.

Thallus: Forming densely short branched pale yellowish-green upright tufts less than 5cm long. The base of the holdfast is not blackened and the inner cord is white.

Apothecia: None.

Chemistry: No lichen tests. Contains usnic acid.

Similar Species: There are 79 species of *Usnea* in North America. Many beard lichens, when young, can be mistaken with Bristly Beard Lichen. Be certain to look closely at the attachment to the substrate. Other species may drape from twigs or have a dark black base at the point of attachment.

Powdered Beard Lichen *Usnea lapponica*

Grows on branches of conifers.

trees

Description: Fruticose pale yellowish-green main stems rooted to the substrate with many rounded or dented side branches.

Thallus: Forms a pale yellowish-green shrubby tuft less than 8cm long with rounded or dented branches covered with small bumps and powder. The base is usually pale with a white inner cord.

Apothecia: None.

Chemistry: May be PD+ yellow (salazanic and usnic acids).

Similar Species: Boreal Oakmoss (*Evernia mesomorpha*) is thicker and lacks the soredia. Bushy Lichens (*Ramalina*) are all flattened branches.

Nature Notes:

Soredia (the powder on the branches) are vegetative reproductive structures. Each tiny granule is actually a ball of fungal tissue enveloping a portion of the photosynthetic partner. As the soredia are brushed from the lichen thallus, they blow away and become lodged in the bark of a suitable tree to grow into a new lichen.

fruticose

Boreal Beard Lichen *Usnea subfloridana*

Grows mainly on spruce in coniferous forests.

trees

Nature Notes:

Fishbone Beard Lichen (*Usnea filipendula*) has been used in the far east of Russia in the powdered form to treat wounds. Recent tests have shown positive antibacterial activity. Although presently there are few commercial uses of lichen substances, the variety of antibacterial properties makes them very interesting for continued study. A fair amount of research has been focused on the value of usnic acid. This compound is present in *Usnea*.

fruticose

Description: Fruticose pale yellowish-green shrubby or drooping main stems with several slender main branches.

Thallus: Pale yellowish-green shrubby or draping main branches less than 15cm long with fairly abundant side branches. The base of the holdfast is blackened while the central cord is white. The tips of branches are not wavy.

Apothecia: Rare.

Chemistry: UV+ blue-white (squamitic acid).

Similar Species: Fishbone Beard Lichen (*Usnea filipendula*) is strictly draping and the branches have wavy tips. The medulla is PD+ yellow and K+ red due to presence of salazanic acid.

Methuselah's Beard Lichen   *Usnea longissima*

Grows at the tops of spruce or fir trees in humid cedar swamps often near lakes or streams.

trees

Description: Fruticose with very long pale yellowish-green main stems with many relatively short side branches.

Thallus: Pale yellowish-green long draping main stems 15-30cm long (possibly up to 3m long) with equal side branching 3-40mm long. It is not attached to the substrate, but rather drapes over branches. The central cord is pinkish to brown.

Apothecia: Rare.

Chemistry: No positive tests. Substances include evernic, barbatic and diffractaic acids.

Similar Species: Pitted Beard Lichen (*Usnea cavernosa*) has a similar growth form but is significantly shorter with unequal side branches and distinct pitting in the main stem.

Nature Notes:

This species is one of the most pollution-sensitive lichens in the North Woods. Populations in Europe have all but completely disappeared. Since air quality has not been shown to be an issue in much of our region, the main threat to this species' survival in the North Woods is logging of old growth forests. Populations on Isle Royale are likely secure. It is one of 11 species recognized as a species of concern in the North Woods.

Reproduction is by fragmentation.

It was likely the original tinsel on Christmas trees.

fruticose

Pitted Beard Lichen   *Usnea cavernosa*

Draping from the branches of spruce in well-lit boreal forests.

Nature Notes:

A native culture in California tanned leather with this beard lichen by wrapping the brains of the animal in the lichen and then rubbing and crumbling it into the hide.

Northern Parulas, (a species of warbler) construct their nests of this draping lichen. In areas of high air pollution, this important nesting material is at risk...and so are the baby Northern Parulas.

Description: Fruticose with long pale yellowish-green draping main stems with few perpendicular side branches.

Thallus: Pale yellowish-green long draping stems 10-40cm long with mostly long and unequal side branches. The main stem is constricted at the nodes, has distinct pitting and there is no holdfast.

Apothecia: Uncommon.

Chemistry: Medulla PD+ Yellow and K+ yellow turning to red (salazinic acid).

Similar Species: The rare Methusaleh's Beard Lichen (*Usnea longissima*) has equal branching. It is often much longer and grows in humid sites. It is also possible to confuse *Usnea cavernosa* with Angel's Hair (*Ramalina thrausta*), another rare lichen found growing on trees and bushes in wet habitats. Angel's Hair lacks a central cord and cleanly breaks when pulled.

trees

fruticose

Glossary

Algae: A photosynthetic organism.

Apothecia: A disk or cup-shaped structure that produces spores for the mycobiont.

Areole: A small, irregular patch of thallus.

Ascomycete: A fungus that produces its spores within a sac-like structure called an ascus. These fungi include disk or cup fungi.

Axil: The joint between two lobes.

Basidiomycete: A fungus that produces its spores as external buds on club-like structures. These fungi are often the typical mushrooms we see with a stalk and cap.

Boreal: A northern forest type where temperatures fall below -41C and the dominant trees are fir, spruce and birch.

Bryophyte: Mosses, liverworts and hornworts. They often grow in habitats similar to lichens.

C test: A spot test for identification purposes; sodium hypochlorite or undiluted household bleach is used as the reagent.

Calcareous: Rock or soil rich in calcium carbonate; may be limestone, dolomite, marble, sandstone or other rock that reacts (fizzing) to HCl.

Cephalodia: A small growth occurring on or in some lichens (esp *Pelitigera*) that contains cyanobacteria.

Chemotype: A division of like species based on chemistry.

Cilia: Hair-like appendages found on the edges of the thallus or apothecia.

Cortex: The outer layer of a lichen composed of fungal tissue.

Corticolous: Growing on bark.

Crustose: A lichen growth form in such close contact with its substrate that it may resemble spray paint.

Cyanobacteria: A photosynthetic bacteria also called blue-green algae.

Cyphellae: A specialized pore in a lichen thallus providing gas exchange.

Endolithic: Growth of a lichen literally within the rock crystalline matrix.

Endophloeodal: Growth of a lichen within the surface layers of tree bark.

Foliose: A lichen growth form that looks more or less leafy.

Fruticose: A lichen growth form that is shrubby; it can be stalked, draping or tufted.

Fungi: An organism without chlorophyll that reproduces by spores and lives by absorbing nutrients from organic matter.

Heath: A vegetation type common in nutrient-poor northern wetlands composed of plants of Ericaeae (leatherleaf, Labrador tea, cranberry, blueberry, etc).

Holdfast: A relatively thick lichen attachment point to a substrate as in *Umbilicaria* and some *Usnea*.

Hyphae: Fungal filaments.

Isidia: A tiny growth containing photobiont cells surrounded by cortex; this growth serves as a vegetative reproductive structure.

K test: A spot test for identification purposes; a ten percent potassium hydroxide solution or Liquid Plumber is used as the reagent.

KC test: A spot test for identification purposes; one drop of K is then followed by one drop of C.

Lichen: A symbiotic association with a mycobiont (fungus) and a photobiont (algae or cyanobacteria).

Lichenized: Referring to the fungus having a relationship with an algae, cyanobacteria or both.

Lichenometry: The study of dating surfaces and thus events using knowledge of lichen growth rates and size.

Lobe: A flattened branch or projection from the main thallus.

Macrolichen: A foliose or fruticose lichen; positive identification may be achieved with little use of microscopy.

Medulla: The internal layer of a thallus composed of loosely packed fungal hyphae.

Microlichen: A crustose lichen; positive identification must utilize the tools of microscopy.

Mycobiont: The fungal partner in a lichen.

Nostoc: A genus of cyanobacteria found in many lichen associations;

its presence can be detected by the dark brown, black or grey color of the lichen thallus.

Outcrop: Area of bedrock projecting above the soil.

PD test: A spot test for identification purposes; paraphenylenediamine is dissolved in 5-10 ml of ethyl alcohol.

Photobiont: The photosynthetic partner in a lichen; either algae or cyanobacteria.

Photosynthesis: The process in which organisms containing the green substance chlorophyll use the energy from sunlight to produce carbohydrates.

Podetia: A hollow stalk common in *Cladonia*; they can be a variety of shapes with or without an apothecial disk at the top.

Pseudocyphellae: Tiny breaks in the cortex serving in the exchange of gases; they are often the color of the medulla.

Rhizines: Root-like structures serving to attach the lower cortex of foliose lichens to the substrate; rhizines can vary in length, thickness, color and branching.

Saxicolous: Growing on rock, stone, pebbles, concrete, brick or like substances.

Siliceous: Rock or soil rich in silica; may be granite, gneiss, quartz, basalt, rhyolite or other rock which does not react with HCl.

Soralia: Area of the thallus in which a mass of soredia are formed as in *Peltigera didactyla*.

Soredia: A tiny growth containing photobiont cells wrapped in fungal tissue; this growth serves as a vegetative reproductive structure.

Squamulose: A lichen growth form that looks scale-like; commonly referred to as foliose or crustose.

Substrate: That surface on which the lichen grows although rarely serving the lichen any nutrition.

Symbiosis: A long-term association between two very different organisms; mutualism and parasitism result in a marked change in one or both organisms.

Talus: A sloping deposit of large, angular fragments of rock, usually at the base of a cliff or steep slope.

Terricolous: Growing on the ground including soil, moss and decaying trees.

Thallus: A vegetative body composed of both the photobiant and mycobiont.

Trebouxia: A genus of single-celled green algae common among lichen associations and rarely grows otherwise.

Trentepohlia: A genus of filamentous green algae common in crustose lichen associations; unlichenized individuals often have a distinct orange-red pigment (look on birch bark).

Umbilicate: Attached by a single holdfast (an umbilicus) to a substrate as in *Umbilicaria*.

UV test: A test for identification purposes; UV (ultraviolet light) can be detected in longwave (365nm) and shortwave (254nm) since it causes some lichen substances to fluoresce.

Appendix A
Titles of Interest

Brodo, I.M., Sharnoff, S.D., and Sharnoff, S. 2001. *Lichens of North America.* Yale University Press, New Haven & London. 795 pp.

Esslinger, T. L. 2006. *A Cumulative Checklist for the Lichen-forming,_Lichenicolous and Allied Fungi of the Continental United States and Canada.* North Dakota State University: http://www.ndsu.nodak.edu/instruct/esslinge/chcklst/chcklst7.htm (First posted 1 December 1997, Most Recent Update 10 April 2006), Fargo, North Dakota.

Hale, M.E., Jr. 1979. *How to Know the Lichens, (2nd edition)* Wm. C. Brown Co., Dubuque, Iowa, 246 pp.

Hale, M.E., Jr. 1983. *The Biology of Lichens, (3rd edition)* Edward Arnold Ltd., London. 190pp.

McCune, B. and Geiser, L. 1997. *Macrolichens of the Pacific Northwest.* Oregon State University Press, Corvallis, 386 pp.

Medlin, J.J. 1996. *Michigan Lichens.* Cranbrook Institute of Science, Bulletin 60: 1-98.

Nash, T.H., III. 1996. *Lichen Biology.* Cambridge University Press, Cambridge. 303pp.

Pope, R. 2005. *Lichens above Treeline.* University Press of New England, Hanover & London. 69pp.

Purvis, W. 2000. *Lichens.* Smithsonian Institution Press, Washington, D.C. 112pp.

Shaw, J. 1987. *John Shaw's Closeups in Nature.* New York, NY: Amphoto.

St. Clair, L. 1999. *Lichens of the Rocky Mountains.* Brigham Young University, 242pp.

Wetmore, C. M. 2005 (most recent revision). *Keys to the Lichens of Minnesota.* University of Minnesota, St. Paul, Minnesota. 92 pp. Available at http://www.tc.umn.edu/%7Ewetmore/Herbarium/HERB-HOME.htm

Appendix B
Lichen Groups & Websites

American Bryological and Lichenological Society (ABLS)
ABLS publishes both The Bryologist (research papers and reviews) and
Evansia (less technical articles)

http://www.unomaha.edu/abls/

International Association for Lichenology (IAL)
http://www.lichenology.org/index.html

Lichens of North America
http://www.lichen.com/

Lichens of Wisconsin
https://mywebspace.wisc.edu/jpbennet/web/WisconsinLichens/

Michigan State University Lichen Collection
http://herbarium.msu.edu/lichen.html

Minnesota Lichen Herbarium Home
http://www.tc.umn.edu/%7Ewetmore/Herbarium/HERBHOME.htm

NPLichen: A Database of Lichens in the U.S. National Parks
http://www.ies.wisc.edu/nplichen/

Ontario Ministry of Natural Resources—Lichen species list
http://nhic.mnr.gov.on.ca/MNR/nhic/species/species_list.cfm

Wisconsin Lichens
http://www.botany.wisc.edu/wislichens/index.html

Appendix C
Photo Credits

All photos are by the author except those listed below.

Stephen Sharnoff: 1b, 2, 36, 49, 51, 63, 68ab, 74, 93, 98, 100ab, 104, 109, 114, 117, 119, 125, 127, 139.

Sparky Stensaas (www.stoneridgepress.com): cover (main), 6, 8, 11c, 15b, 59b, 83c.

Index

Other user-friendly field guides from Kollath-Stensaas Publishing

**Dragonflies
of the
North Woods**

ISBN
0-9673793-6-9

**Damselflies
of the
North Woods**

ISBN
0-9673793-7-7

**Spiders
of the
North Woods**

ISBN
0-9673793-4-2

**Butterflies
of the
North Woods**

ISBN
0-9673793-8-5